ONE BRIEF RUN

By:

David Trout Pomeroy

Dedicated to my editors.

One Brief Run
Preface

Brittle and yellowing, they reside in file drawers in a room in a building in a small city where many of them flashed across the realm of public attention as newspaper articles. They number in the thousands and reflect one weird person's brief (ten-year) run as a reporter/columnist/music critic/feature writer. Their significance in American cultural history is unmistakable and easily forgiven. They rest now, in the darkness of files rarely opened. They're kept on the premise the person who wrote all the articles might want to read them again, time allowing. They're organized by newspaper; he wrote for several of them, not counting the wire services and the tabloids that didn't last and the hippie papers out in California, where all he wrote translates now as certifiable gobble-dee-gook. Some articles were slightly rewritten by editors who exercised their prerogatives with a mixture of grumbling and cursing. Others sailed directly from the writer's computer to the bottom of the reader's parakeet cage.

Many years after this demented person's career as a newspaper writer came to an end, he took it upon himself to identify and gather the specific pieces from this melange of thin paper and fading ink that he felt best exemplified the era from which they came. Once done, he pondered his decisions, second-guessed many selections, found others, held them to the light and settled upon the collection assembled herein, here here. This did not contribute to better mental health. Rather, he trembled at the thought something worthwhile might still be inadvertently left out. Or an included piece might not be as worthy as thought in the quiet hours of an elderly writer's morning. Soon his anxiety led to fits of sheer paranoid rambling, giving way eventually to loud sobbing in the most unlikely of venues, including his own libido. From this convulsed journey into the psychological unknown emerged the collection, "One Brief Run," a spectacular leap of egocentric proportion. I hope like hell you like it. Clearly, I did. If I didn't think so much of these articles, I'd keep them in the file until my retirement, now scheduled for either four or 40 years from now. It's not the writing, mind you, it's the subject matter. I believe anyone could have written any this garbage. I just happened to get the assignments. They were good ones. I was lucky.

David Trout Pomeroy
Pontiac, Michigan – 2003

A legend on his own time

Rip said he'd be over in about 10 minutes. So I waited.

An hour later, he hadn't appeared. Still I waited. Rip Watkins had cast a spell upon me. I was under his power and was willing to wait for him for over an hour.

Rip had told me he'd get a special radio antenna I needed.

Then, when I stopped by his store to pick it up, his brother, Major, told me Rip wasn't working at the time. He was, Major reported, at home, so we called him on the phone.

Rip said he'd be over in 10 minutes. And then he took his time.

First, Rip told us, he'd have to "Stop at the warehouse" to pick up the right model antenna. That sounded fairly reasonable. Stop by the warehouse. I imagined it was located in a modern industrial park outside Waterford.

Later, Major told me what that meant.

"Ya," he said, "that's Rip's catch-all line: 'I got that at the warehouse.' It could mean anything. What he calls 'at his warehouse' could be anywhere you could think of. He might have to stop for it somewhere, but it ain't gonna be no warehouse."

Finally Rip showed up, bursting with a huge smile into the dusty darkness of the showroom of his TV repair store. What began as an ostensible "10 minutes" had become more than an hour. That made Rip chuckle, and within moments, the three of us were standing there laughing about it.

"He's always been this way," Major had explained to me during our long wait for his phantom brother.

"Guys that's known him 15-20 years will all tell you that. They just accept it. They don't hold it against him…it's just the way he is. If there's something he don't want to do, he can procrastinate like you can't believe."

Rip, I finally guessed, was one of those completely irresponsible guys who – through some means or another – are able to get away with living that way.

"He's got certain defense tactics," Major explained as we stood near a row of dated black-and-white TV's, talking wine and women and waiting for his brother.

"Among those who know him, he's a legend," Major said.

Major's stories about his brother began warming up nicely.

Rip – it was becoming evident – was Pontiac's answer to Fred Sanford. I found a pencil.

"Rip's quite an unusual character," said Major, who installs burglar alarms for a living.

"As a businessman, he's amazing. It's almost like he makes a living by accident. I know he could make three times as much money if he ever made up his mind he wanted to."

Instead, Rip procrastinates. Or snoozes.

"One time he fell asleep in his car while he was pulled up at some railroad tracks, waiting for a train," Major recalled. "This guy came running in here and said, 'Hey!, Go wake up your brother, he's got traffic lined up all the way back to the golf course.'"

Major and I got something of a roar over that one.

"I'm sure he's got anxieties, just like everyone else but I don't know about them," Major said with authority. "The man's a character."

"He can fix a TV just about as good as anybody around here," Major said. "He's got an ego thing about it. He's at his best when people bring him sets that other shops can't fix – when he's in his prime."

I was beginning to understand the power of Rip Watkins.

"In the old days, Rip could really stall," Major said. "Like when we were kids and had to do the dishes, Rip would do just about anything he could to get out of it.

"Then, on those nights when he'd finally had to face up to it, he'd just leave the water runnin' so it sounded like he was washing and then he'd fall asleep leaning on the oven door. If it's something he don't want to do, he can really procrastinate."

That sounded familiar.

"Some of our brothers still say that sleeping on the oven door baked Rip's brains out but I don't think so," Major theorized.

"If it had, he wouldn't be able to work on those TV circuits the way he does."

Rip works all night in his cluttered back shop sometimes, his stubby cigar always in place.

"He does better at night," Major said. "It's easier tracing all those circuits when the phone's not always ringing."

That's how Rip can act like a loser and still be a winner, I realized.

Like everyone else, the man just needs his space.

Incidentally, the price was right on the antenna.

An artist in motion – just like his work

Color him gone.

George Vihos, and Oakland County artist whose works are known throughout the country, moved last week from his hilltop lair off Lake Angelus Road in Auburn Hills to the Salinas Valley in California.

Vihos, 47, established a national reputation for what critics have called his "Images of Flight," brushstroked drawings with feathery curves that suggest the movement of intricate birds in flight.

Vihos has been in motion, too. He has called New York, Auburn Hills and California home during recent years. Finally, he has settled on Salinas as his permanent base to paint and create new markets.

"Californians aren't necessarily interested in contemporary art," Vihos says, "but they are receptive."

Meeting someone in Michigan, Vihos admits, generally evokes a predictive response: "Oh, you paint." In California, a new acquaintance is more likely to be a future "collaborator."

"Out there they find out what I'm doing, and there's a greater likelihood that it may be related somehow to what they may be doing."

On a muggy morning last week, the final brushes and pastels were packed and ready in the front room of Viho's rented home – a rare remnant of hand-hewn living space that was built by Scottish settlers over 160 years ago.

The studio in all its antiquity overlooks the new General Motors assembly plant in Orion Township and the perpetual I-75 traffic jams below.

Vihos spent his final Michigan days packing and exchanging yarns with close friends, including Pontiac painter Frank Safranek and his son Tim, chair designer- builder Jose Ruguerio and Vihos' former agent in Birmingham, Lee Hoffman.

Oakland Community College artist Ray Katz organized a going-away party for Vihos, which was a success even though Vihos could not attend at the last minute.

"Everyone understood," Safranek said. "We had a hell of a good party for him, even without him. We knew he had something else to do. It wasn't a big deal to us."

The last weekend passed slowly.

"Leaving hasn't been an easy decision," Vihos says. "I could have stayed here indefinitely."

Vihos was raised by Greek parents in Detroit, nurtured by the Detroit Institute of Arts, educated in Chicago at that city's Art Institute and University of Chicago.

"I never graduated from high school," Vihos says, recalling a heartbroken father who didn't quite understand. "I was always running around down at Arts & Crafts (now the Center for Creative Studies) trying to learn how to draw."

Until he was in school, Vihos spoke only Greek. His family home was only blocks away from the Detroit Institute of Arts, and as a youngster he would accompany his mother to the institute on a regular basis.

"It was a blessing," he says. "Being there all the time gave me the opportunity to observe. When you can't communicate in a normal way, you look and learn to figure things out with your eyes.

"Visualization had never baffled me at all."

After a stint in the Navy, Vihos worked as an instructor at the Roeper School in Bloomfield Hills, at Wayne State University, Flint Junior College, the Center for Creative Studies and the Bloomfield Art Association.

In the late 1960s, as he was on the verge of becoming one of Michigan's best-known artists, Vihos disappeared from the Michigan art scene, to study on a Fulbright scholarship in Florence, Italy.

By 1970, Vihos had returned to Detroit, but soon started living here part-time and broadening his base to New York City. In recent years, Vihos' work has been exhibited at New York's Metropolitan Museum of Art and his career has become associated more directly with Gotham than Auburn Hills.

His recent accomplishments include:

• A sprawling mural – largeness being a general characteristic of Vihos' work – is on its way to the

governor's mansion in Lansing from the Detroit Institute of Arts.

- Another Vihos work now occupies the north entranceway to the Wayne State University Medical School.

- Yet another Vihos is on the wall in the main entranceway of Detroit's Receiving Hospital.

"I love to make art. It's what I do best," Vihos says. "Up until now, outside Manhattan, Michigan is the place where people make things."

For some years, Vihos said, the New York to Detroit pattern made the most sense. Now California – with its rich potential for support and collaboration – must become part of the nexus.

When he first saw the countryside surrounding Salinas – 70miles south of San Francisco – Vihos realized that a strong resemblance exists between his early work and the verdant hillsides in northern California.

"We were standing on our deck in the morning, looking at this beautiful setting, and I said to my wife, 'Look at this. I painted this in Michigan.'"

Bloomfield Township meeting is Homer Case's last hurrah

Rubbing his hands in anticipation and waving his gavel playfully, retiring Township Supervisor Homer Case officiated his final township board meeting Monday night.

First elected to his position in 1963, Case has served as the township's fourth supervisor.

Men named Arno Hulet, David Anderson and Perry Vaughan preceded him. A man named Fred Korzon will follow.

In between there has been the 25-year reign of Homer Case.

"Thanks for the memories," his friends sang to him at a recent retirement party, including the lyrics:

"Those township's growing pains, and all your highest aims, the zoning board, the growing hordes of people that complain, how lovely it was…"

Something of that spirit existed at Case's final meeting as supervisor Monday night. Trustees escorted him into the township auditorium, a few minutes before the meeting time, doting over the retiring boss.

"I can't see that clock back there," Case asked as he called the meeting to order. "Is it 8 o'clock yet?"

It was and Case began zipping through his final agenda.

After approving previous board minutes, Case announced the appointment of Dennis McGee as new Deputy Chief of the police department.

"I'll let your wife pin these on you," Case told McGee, holding the officer's new badges.

"I don't want to put a hole in your suit."

Case posed for a picture with McGee and the officer's wife and drew a laugh from the audience as he pulled in his trousers, with the assistance of Township Clerk Deloris Little.

"That's why we have a woman on the board," she said.

Speaking in a low, monotone voice, Case then marched through a succession of special assessment district closings, eliciting unanimous votes of approval on each measure.

"That's all of 'em, right?" he asked at the conclusion of the sequence.

A township resident appeared before the board to appeal an estimated sewer-water billing. He had been a victim of a faulty water meter, the resident told Case.

"I had a leak in my meter once, and had to pay a $140 repair bill," Case informed the resident. "I know. I've been here 25 years and a water meter's never overcharged."

The resident later resumed his argument.

"I don't think you understand," he told Case.

"I understand you perfectly," the retiring supervisor said. "I've been here too long."

Other board members, including Ms. Little and designate- supervisor Korzon, picked up the discussion with the resident as Case swung around in his swivel chair, turning his back to the audience during the remainder of the discussion.

Trustee Bill Yaw ultimately struck a compromise solution with the resident. Then Case returned once again to his job.

"Fire reports," he said.

"Let's see…we haven't built anything and we haven't burnt anything down."

And that was that for fire reports.

The township board meeting of Dec. 28 was cancelled.

Bob Seger – After years on the road, he's the 'gorilla' of rock

The motorcycle appeared, a huge BMW 530, sliding gracefully east on Baldwin Road. As it rolled closer, the driver's face revealed a remarkable grin behind mustache, beard, goggles and helmet. Both motorcycle and man seemed driven by forces remarkable and huge across northern Oakland County hills.

Driving the motorcycle was Robert Clark Seger, 33, Oakland County's internationally known rock star. Minutes before, Seger had sound checked his microphones and amplifiers at nearby Pine Knob. Now, he was wheeling toward his Clarkston home to change clothes and prepare for the opening night of his 1978 hometown stand.

For the thousands of fans fortunate enough to attend any of his seven late summer Pine Knob concerts, the remarkable grin from the man atop the BMW was easily explainable. They would see him on stage, riding the crest of a brilliant musical career, exuding an extraordinary sense of happiness, an outward display of joy so apparent as to be visible from beneath a fast-moving motorcycle helmet.

"More than any rock star I know," Waterford-bred critic Dave Marsh says, "Bob Seger has earned his peace of mind."

"You should have seen it," a young parking attendant raved at the back Pine Knob gate, only minutes after Seger had breezed across Baldwin Road that late August night. "Bob Seger himself, on this killer BMW. He just rode right out of here. Said he'd be back in an hour."

Trained to deal with all extremes, the stunned attendant wavered slightly before asking, "Do you believe it?"

Bob Seger has become a global phenomenon through his believability. In 1978, that believability separates him from the rest of the pack, with the exception only, perhaps, of Bruce Springsteen, the New Jersey rock sensation with whom Seger is most frequently – and odiously – compared.

Seger's distinct artistry, sentimental and optimistic, has developed through the years to a point of absolute purity. Seger is 15 fine years into a slow-paced, but never- less-than-promising rock music career, what promoter Bill Graham would call a "monster" star. Or, as People magazine called Detroit's oldest sensation this summer, a "gorilla" star.

Seger, the gorilla, has a rock 'n' roll head and a rock 'n' roll heart. Combined with a superb lyrical talent, snazzy showmanship and the most hard-thrusting five-man band in all of Motorland, the current Seger system represents rock 'n' roll succeeding late in the 1970s.

Before disk jockey Alan Freed began using the expression on the radio in Cleveland in the early 1950s, "rock 'n' roll" was strictly black street slang for sexual intercourse. Freed renamed rhythm and blues, which white audiences regarded as being "race music." Freed called it "rock and roll."

Since then, America and the western world have integrated this disparate musical form – rock 'n' roll – to the point at which it may be bigger than all of us. If mainstream interests in rock 'n' roll have wavered slightly during its stormy 30 years, it hasn't been the fault of Bob Seger. Since his first recording in 1961 at age 15, Seger, a Ann Arbor native, has exalted it, inspiring his fans – first in Detroit, later throughout the Midwest, and now from East L.A. to West Bombay and all the way to Katmandu.

Seger was born in Detroit, May 6, 1945, the son of a safety worker at the Ford River Rouge plant who also played clarinet. His family moved to Ann Arbor six years later. When he was 10, his father left home. Bob's 14-year-old brother helped support the family. His mother worked as a housekeeper.

Growing up in Ann Arbor, Seger listened to WLAC, Nashville's powerful rhythm and blues station, imbuing the soul sound of Wilson Pickett, Little Richard and James Brown. In junior high school, he formed his first band, the Decibels. Seger sang lead and held bass.

"I couldn't play and sing at the same time then," he now admits. "So I'd just stand up front, singing with the bass in my hand."

Eventually the Decibels played fraternity parties at the nearby University of Michigan, across the street from Ann Arbor High School. Seger switched to lead guitar and the band played additional gigs at strip joints, bowling alleys, and local cocktail lounges.

In 1963, Seger, along with 700 others, graduated from Ann Arbor High School. He claims that until he discovered girls and rock 'n' roll he'd been a jock and an honor student. "After that I barely graduated with a D average," he says.

"You would never have confused him with an honor student," Skip Hopp, one of Seger's classmates at the time recalls. "He was quite regular. One of the boys. Not a jock and not a brain. I didn't even think he was into music that much. He was just there."

Fifteen years later, Ann Arbor High School's class of 1963 organized a reunion. Prominent on their list of grads who could not be found was Bob Seger's name.

Has anyone ever heard of him?

Before his eleventh album, "Stranger in Town," was released this past spring, over one million copies had already been ordered from around the world.

Surely someone knows where Bob Seger is.

He would have been hard to lose track of after 1963. After all, he stayed in Ann Arbor, playing in bands, making records and becoming what one writer called "sort of a Midwestern wunderkind."

After graduation, more gigging and a few rudimentary recording efforts, Seger successfully introduced a handful of local singles like "Heavy Music," and "Persecution Smith." He met his current manager, Punch Andrews, at an Ypsilanti bowling alley in 1965. Their first release together was "East-Side Story," which sold 50,000 records, mostly in Michigan. Later, with Andrews, Seger released another regional hit "2&2=?", a hard rock anti-war song that questioned, "I'm not a prophet…all I'm asking is why I've got to die?"

The single, "Ramblin', Gamblin' Man" became the name of his first album as well as his first national hit single in 1969. For the next several years, with various bands, Seger continued to tour the Midwest.

They played one-night stands. They opened for other bands. They performed Detroit's radically energetic rock and roll for as many as 250 nights per year.

During these years, Seger played nearly every rock club in southeastern Michigan, all of which are long since closed. In Detroit it was the Cinderella, the Grande, the East Town. In Birmingham, the Palladium. In Royal Oak, it was the Farmer's Market. In Clawson, The Hideout. In Pontiac, it was the Firebird Lounge. Near Lake Orion, the Silver Bell. He played Mt. Holly Ski Lodge for years and entered every battle of the bands that ever was, personifying the Detroit rock scene.

Mary Beth Kocsis, 26, of Pontiac, says, "Like most Michigan rockers, he didn't have much stage presence then. It didn't matter. Most people just sat and listened anyway. His music was enough."

During his recent seven-night stint at Pine Knob in Clarkston, a few minutes by motorcycle from his nearby modest ranch-type home, Seger's music continued to provide all that was necessary for an outstanding evening. As an international star, though, he definitely brought something extra.

As is still the case, Seger didn't earn any more money than the other musicians in his band. "I think everyone goes through the same amount of road torture," he once said. Seger's democratic standards limited the effectiveness of his early bands, he now realizes, explaining, "Everybody wanted something different." Divergence equaled diffusion as his bands tried too much of everything and not enough of anything specific.

Which, as success neared, was to become, increasingly, the distilled specificity of their natural leader Bob Seger.

While his band attempted too broad a range of contemporary material, Seger also over-extended himself, trying to play lead and sing lead vocals at once, ala Eric Clapton. "That was the worst thing that happened to me," he told WABX-FM's Jerry Lubin last month. "I just got blown away by lead guitar for about four years. I stopped being a songwriter and stopped being creative."

It was when Seger began concentrating on his writing again that national attention began concentrating on his music. His first slow ballad, "Turn the Page," was released with the album "Back in '72," in 1972. The instant classic "Katmandu" followed. All were big hits, yet still on a mostly regional level.

By 1972, however, Seger had turned the page. His band played strictly Seger's material, revealing the greater scope of his lyrical promise.

Seger's next page began during a conversation with his old friend from Royal Oak, Glenn Frey.

During the 1960s, both had played in clubs managed by Punch Andrews. Frey ended up in Los Angeles, becoming a millionaire with the preeminent rock group, The Eagles.

It was Frey who called Seger on the telephone in 1967, instructing Bob to "Come over and hear this album!" The album was a psychedelic breakthrough called "Are You Experienced!" by Jimi Hendrix.

"Oh, oh, we're dated," Seger remembers them thinking as they listened together. Because of this historic episode, Seger played lead guitar until 1972.

At one point, Seger and Frey tried writing songs together. It didn't work. "We were like two trains coming at each other," Seger told WABX's Lubin. As it was, their friendship didn't suffer. Frey visited Seger in Michigan; Seger visited Frey in Los Angeles. In 1974, when Seger was preparing his eighth album, Frey arrived again. Seger shared with him his latest tapes, including many ballads.

Frey advised Seger, "Go with them, man. Do something diverse." Seger used the slower material, including "Jody Girl" and "Beautiful Loser," also the title cut of the album.

"Beautiful Loser," released in 1975, was Seger's first effort with his current backup group, The Silver Bullet Band. It represented another giant step toward national acclaim.

Featuring Drew Abbot, formerly of a Detroit band called Third Power, on lead guitar, with horns played by Alto Reed, The Silver Bullet Band have come to complement Seger's sound with a perfect, seemingly made in heaven ensemble presence.

In addition, Skip Knape, formerly of Ann Arbor's Teargarden and Van Winkle, plays drums, and Robyn Robbins, once of a well-known local group called Frost, handles keyboards. Chris Campbell balanced the Silver Bullet effect on bass.

Knape – as Van Winkle – was master of ceremonies at the most crazed event of all time in Michigan, the 1970 Goose Lake rock festival. Onstage today, the entire band continues to embody the festival spirit, with Alto Reed, pumping saxophone solos, guitarist Abbott stunning with brilliant leads, and Robbins Campbell, and Knape sustaining the sound.

With the Silver Bullet Band, "Beautiful Loser" became a gorgeous winner.

"That album got me through cooking mess in the Navy," says Raleigh Fontaine, one of many Oakland County Seger- lovers. "He took seriously the pathos and aspirations of the man on the street. He didn't necessarily provide any answers, but his statements at least helped you feel better."

With "Beautiful Loser" earning wide attention and outselling all his previous albums, Seger and band released a double-album, "Live Bullet," expanding his commercial momentum. Later, in 1977, Seger's first absolute smash LP, "Night Moves," followed, crystallizing his national stature. Fifteen months later, Seger's latest effort, "Stranger in Town," arrived, solidifying the crystallization.

Bob Seger, quite unsuddenly, is the hottest star in sight. In Michigan, he's so popular that he can't go out in public. He craves his privacy as much as his recognition. "It's tough to go out anymore," he says. "In Detroit, it's impossible. Onstage you want to be the center of attention. Offstage you want to be just another human being, but people always expect more."

So Seger plays it cool in Clarkston, living with girlfriend Jan, practicing with his band, writing new songs, and proceeding with the constant process of either preparing for or recovering from tours. When asked, he says he stays in the Detroit area for one simple reason: "It's a great rock 'n' roll city."

Those around him claim Seger is essentially unaffected by fame.

"Everyone wants interviews," Seger's Andrews says. "The Oakland Press, the Free Press, the News, the Flint Journal…we just don't physically have the time for them.

"Besides," he adds, "Bob's heard the same questions so often that now he's starting making up new answers."

Church honors couple on 60th wedding anniversary

Bennie Townsend was alone at the reins of a four-horse wagon, hauling a load of logs down main street in Peach Orchard, Ark., when he first spotted Eva – the woman who would become his wife – walking along the sidewalk.

The year was 1920.

For Bennie, as in many a wonderful fairy tale, it was love at first site.

"That's where I found this beautiful girl," he gushed recently, playfully nudging his bride of 60 years. "She looked good then and she looks good now."

For Eva Townsend, the ardor wasn't quite as immediate.

"I thought he was kind of fresh at first," she said and laughed. "He gave me this smile and I wasn't sure what to do."

"She smiled right back," Bennie grinned.

Something clicked. The couple was married in Arkansas a year later. Sixty years later, their flirting continues.

This was proven when The Faith Baptist Church of Auburn Heights recently held a celebration on the occasion of the couple's 60th wedding anniversary.

In spite of a kidney infection and a slight trace of pneumonia, 88-year-old Bennie Townsend and his spry wife Eva, 76, were the life of their own party, embracing guests and kidding with each other throughout a beautiful night.

Bennie Townsend is the grand patriarch of his congregation. During the 1940s, in fact, he helped dig the footings of the current church building at 3931 Auburn, near Adams Road, in Auburn Heights.

Bennie holds the original church blueprints.

So it comes as no surprise that the Faith Baptist Church congregation turned out in large numbers to help the couple celebrate their recent anniversary.

Don Evilsizer, the church's minister, was there to bless the cake and ice cream, as was Edith Rowe, the church member who organized the event. Both beamed with excitement.

The Townsend's son Bob and his wife Betty were there, as were church member Emory Childers and his sons Mark and Todd. Another family friend, Max Lee, sat near the Townsends as the group celebrated the occasion with a evening of photographers, gift giving and spirited fellowship.

Church members had chipped in their funds to buy Bennie and Eva the one item they wanted most – a tub encloser- shower addition for their new home. The Townsend's old home on Eastwood Road burned to the ground more than a year ago. Son Bob has been building his parents a new home on the same site.

Seated proudly before the church group, the Townsends shared the secret of their successful years together.

"We've simply worked together, 50-50, and done our best to try and get along," Bennie said. "Even when I was down to nothing, she's stuck with me. She was always willing to bear the same burdens I had to. We've just always said, 'Where there's a will, there's a way.' We've been way up and we've been way down but we stuck it out."

There were many trials to endure.

After their marriage in "the backwoods of Arkansas," the Townsends moved to Missouri, where Bennie continued to work in the lumbering business. When a cyclone hit that area in 1926 and "tore the town all to pieces," the Townsends came north to Michigan, settling in Auburn Heights.

Bennie says there were only 20 homes in the village at that time.

His first job was for the government, picking up corn stalks in area farm fields. Later he worked construction jobs, helped plant shade trees on South Boulevard and eventually took a position at Fisher Body.

Bennie's starting pay in the late 1920s was 50 cents an hour. When he retired from the plant in 1956, his hourly wage had increased to $2.46.

From 1943-1969, Eva did assembly work at GMC Truck and Coach.

Today the couple lives with their son, Bob, and his wife, Betty, as their new home nears completion. Bennie – who continued working eight hours a day at odd jobs up until last summer – applies his energy now to the preservation of a ¾-acre vegetable garden in his son's backyard.

With three children, 14 grandchildren and eight great grandchildren living in the area, the Townsends are rarely alone.

Even we they are alone, they still have each other.

Her first day on the job

Seventeen-year-old Faye Kinsel started her first job last week. She had decided to become a waitress. Then she became one.

Based on one day's experience, it looks as though she'll be a good one.

Faye started her job around 11 a.m. on a Monday. Her first customer was a middle-aged man. Her first order was for a Coneydog, without onions.

"One Coney, without," she tried to shout to Bill Grannis, the cook at Jimmy's Coney Island in Avon Township's Meadowbrook Village Mall – where the story of her first day in the work-a-day world was unfolding.

The words, unfortunately, barely came out of her mouth.

Faye Kinsel – whose home is in Waterford and whose smile could stop an army – was so nervous she could hardly write out her first-ever order.

There she was, though, tentatively sticking her toe in the water of her first job experience. It was quite a moment.

On her eternally significant first day of work, Faye was lucky. All three of the other waitresses who were working at Jimmy's that morning pitched in to help their new workmate learn the tricks of effective waitressing.

This is the way it should be on the first days for all first-time ever workers. Faye's co-workers deserve automatic passage to heaven for the decency beyond the call of duty they showed on Faye's first day.

It was touching.

"OK, you had one hot tea, right?," the girls said.

"So you get a pot down from up here and use these cups over here. The tea bags are in this case and you get the hot water out of this dispenser."

Faye would have been lost without this help. Then, by the time she was ready to call in her second-ever order, she was better prepared.

The other girls had been coaching her.

At first, they called out her orders with her, slowly repeating the lines together. As they coached, Faye stood quietly listening to them, wringing her hands with desperation.

As the others offered instructions, she looked over the sea of hungry faces that were her future customers. A look of profound hopefulness was written upon her frail young face.

But help was on its way. Faye was not alone.

Before she called her next order to the cook, the girls made her practice her lines.

Speaking in whispers so the customers wouldn't hear, they rehearsed kitchen language together.

"One cheeseburger, medium rare…one cheeseburger, medium rare…one cheeseburger, medium-rare…"

Moments later, Faye was ready.

"One cheeseburger, medium rare," she called out to the cook, her voice gaining in confidence.

From that point on, things got better.

Sure, she continued to have trouble figuring out how to work the coffee machine and was absolutely perplexed while trying to find a lost side order of toast. This was especially true when the lunch hour rush accelerated to frenzy-level, leaving the other waitresses too busy with their own customers to further help.

But Faye persisted, as all workers – first-day types and otherwise – must.

At one point, she paused beside a stainless steel case that was filled with desserts. Her freshly-scrubbed face and neatly tied-back hair reflected off its glass. Looking to see if anyone was watching, Faye practiced sliding its sliding doors. Back and forth. Back and forth.

She was progressing.

She couldn't quite pronounce the word, "Souvlaki," even though one of her customers wanted some. Then, a kindly fellow waitress saved the day, staging another impromptu pronunciation workshop with Faye as the two of them stood by the Orange Drink dispenser.

Faye got it straight.

"One souvlaki," she cried out. And one souvlaki there was.

"Faye, you've got another man sitting back there," said a waitress, craning her neck in the direction of a customer who had just seated himself at a rear table.

"Don't forget to take your silver," Faye was reminded.

Clutching her order book anxiously, Faye was off. She ruffled its pages as she walked, trying to gain greater familiarity with its feel before confronting her next customer.

Then she was back. This time she called out an order on her own.

It was an easy one.

"One order of french fries," she exhorted with authority. Faye was on her way.

Sure, there were still the moments when she stood alone behind the counter, fumbling for a pencil in the napkin- filled pockets of her apron, continuing to look as scared as a baby deer in your headlights on any highway.

But Faye was on her way.

She was learning fast. The girls had told her, for example, that a good waitress never picks up a customer's dishes until the customer has left. Faye said she was concentrating on that.

By the time 1:15 p.m. of her first day had arrived, Faye – the veteran waitress – was standing in a group, chatting with the other girls, showing all the assuredness of 12 Terry Bradshaws.

Her arms crossed, she stood in a relaxed pose. Most of the customers had gone. The day's main action was over.

Faye and the other girls traveled about in a moving circle, shuffling their feet and talking.

Moments later, Faye – the instant veteran – released a light yawn.

Another day. Another dollar.

Hillbilly Lost

Catlettsburg. Catlettsburg. How do you spell Catlettsburg?

"Let's see," Junior Fannin begins. "C-a-t-t-...Wait a minute. Let me write her out here." Snatching a TV Guide off the simple formica table separating his covered sofa from an aging and ailing television set, he attempts several versions of Catlettsburg.

Let's see," Fannin begins again and again, jotting in the margins of Wednesday's daytime listings.

"C-a-t-l-e-t-t-s-b-u-r-g," he finally concludes, smiling like a young boy surprising everyone by winning a spelling bee. "That's a hard one," he shyly grins.

Catlettsburg, Ky., a hamlet outside Ashland, across the river from Huntington, W.Va.

Catlettsburg, where boys once swam naked on sun-baked afternoons and later in the day looked into the white-rimmed eyes of fathers who spent the day burrowing in the coal mines.

Catlettsburg, Fannin's hometown, light years away from the truck and coach plant that lured him and thousands like him to Pontiac.

Fannin, 37, traveled those light years as so many others from the Catlettsburgs and the Huntingtons and the Little Rocks in search of something more than a life at the bottom of a coal pit or battling the weeds and sun on a road crew.

Those who joined the northward quest that brought Fannin were seeking the good life that always seems hidden in check book balances, as they sought what they couldn't seem to find in their homeland. They couldn't find it in their gritty coal towns because, they said, they were too busy being poor.

And, while being poor and confused and frustrated with the life that seemed to have been ordained for them, they began the dreams that eventually led them North – to the assembly lines here, to the foundries of Pittsburgh, to factories promising high wages and lifelong serenity everywhere above the belovedly despised Mason-Dixon line.

Fannin's tale – and his dreams – are not radically different from that of almost every coal miner'' son who ended up in Northland.

He was born in a little holler called Bear Creek where his ex-wife Janet also was born – two days before her man. In Bear Creek, just like the script would say, the two were wedded. Then, to celebrate and buttress their symbiosis they moved to Catlettsburg where they spawned a family of their own. They also began spawning the inevitable dreams of their own.

They and their children deserved more – more money, more education, more freedom. They wanted it so badly that after awhile the Jim Beam and the Pabst Blue Ribbon didn't sap the hot-night energy of unfulfilled dreams.

After enough of those nights, Fannin packed his "wife" (from whom he was legally divorced, but on temporary friendly terms) four kids and a minute assortment of possessions into a Greyhound bus and headed North.

The dream had begun.

They were on the slick asphalt of I-75 and heading north. Pontiac and its promising assembly lines were going to be theirs – a realization of an Appalachian vision of the American dream.

"We were poor people," says Fannin, whose real name isn't Junior but is Lindsey Fannin Jr. Sinking into the familiar sofa in his rented flat off Huron Street in Pontiac, he remembers life in Kentucky.

Lindsey Fannin Sr. had been a coal miner in Bear Creek. Every day Junior saw the old man head for the mines with his lunch bucket in hand and futility in his gait.

The old man told his only son, "Get out. Go work in some factory. Don't get no job in the hills."

Fannin listened and escaped to Pontiac before his father died of asthma.

But, unlike a lot of others, Fannin had some northern connections.

His sister and husband were already here. "I told her if there were any jobs up there to give me a call and I'd come," Fannin says.

They called and Fannin and company came. He reported to the shop on a Monday, filled out papers in the morning and started to work on the second shift at 3:30 p.m. on the same day.

It wasn't his first job. Fannin quit school at 17 and went to work at a lumberyard in Catlettsburg for 50 cents an hour. By the time of his Bear Creek marriage, the pay was up to $1.50.

"It was the best I've ever lived," he says. "I made $48 a week and lived like a king off it. That was back when you could take a dollar and buy something with it."

In Pontiac, the couple rented for a few years, then bought a home. Mrs. Fannin got her own car and began working in the shop to help with expenses.

Her new independence – shortly following a hysterectomy – furthered the already lengthy distance between them, according to Fannin. "You can't take a country girl and put her in the city," he said. "She'll go wrong everytime. I think you know what I'm talking about. When she finally got loose, she really took off."

When the Fannins cam to Pontiac in 1969 and he earned $4.38 per hour, he grossed $184 a week. Uncle Sam let him keep nearly two-thirds of his check.

Today, 10 years later, Fannin earns $7.17 per hour. In one recent week he grossed $416. Uncle Sam, the UAW, his credit union, his ex-wife and his ex-lawyer let him keep $145.

"Down in Kentucky you think you'll go to the city, make a lot of money and be a rich man, but you ain't," he says. "All you're doin' is payin' bills."

"I'll tell you what's funny," Fannin says. "You go back home now and the few folks that's left see your new truck and think you really got the money, but you know it belongs to the damn credit union."

Although he curses the institution, Fannin's credit union is central to his happiness. "It'd be hard to go down there," he says. "But up here you can always get a hold of money. It's not a problem. If you got a job at Pontiac Motors, you got good credit anywhere. For $10 down, you can buy anything you want."

Anything except happiness or the fruits of a long-sown dream that was abandoned a few years ago when Fannin finally realized that dreams don't mature with a move or a raise and realities like credit unions and bills and black men holding hands with white women don't change easily.

Maybe the coal mines and Pabst after work weren't so bad after all – at least you knew where the man next to you stood and the roots of generations salved the loneliness of unperfected vision.

"I'd love to (return to Kentucky)," Fannin says, "but I couldn't make the same living down there. Their prices are just as high as ours up here."

So nine years into his industrial dream, Fannin plans to stick it out on the line.

Twenty-one years separate him from the benefits of the UAW's renowned "thirty and out" retirement package. "They say after the first 10, the next 20 go by pretty fast," he says, not altogether convincingly.

"I've lived a rough life," Fannin added, "so I might as well keep it up the rest of the way."

A diehead man at Pontiac Truck and Coach, Fannin works channeling dangerously hot sections of mid-sized chrome moldings as they move mechanically from one machine to another.

"I line 'em up so they'll go straight to the table," he says. "On good days I just sit back, relax and watch the man work the machine."

But some bad days come by like the one recently when, he says, he got "careless" and a piece of steel – heated to 1,000 F. – burned viciously into his arm. Now, since his television set conks out as soon as it warms up, Fannin goes to bed early, gets plenty of sleep, and stays awake at work.

After work, Fannin uses his Chevrolet pickup doing odd hauling jobs for friends. "I wasn't raised to charge people for doing things," he explains. "That's why I haven't got nothin'. It's the hillbilly in me. I'd rather just help a guy." Sometimes, in exchange for his services, he'll accept a few dollars worth of gas or an occasional six-pack.

On weekends, Fannin sees his kids, who live with his former wife Janet in the Pontiac area. He has occasional romances, but complains that they always seem to end up far more troubled than they are worth.

He also frequents the Eagles Club on Montcalm where he shoots pool and drinks Pabst. And, every weekend, he plays cards with his sister, at her house.

Often, his take-home pay is on the line.

"Sometimes," he says, "if I don't watch it, I'll lose all my money and have to borrow a dollar on Monday for cigarettes."

Fannin's 17-year-old son, Robert, is back in Kentucky.

"We don't get along," Fannin says of his son. "He's wild. He runs with the marijuana crowd. Told me he wanted to go down south. I told him he can go whenever he liked. When he said he was ready I drove him down.

"He called a few weeks ago asking if I'd sign for him to buy a motorcycle," Fannin says. "I told him to forget it. He'll be 18 soon."

These days Fannin shares his living room with three cages of hamsters, including babies the size of cigarette filters. "They're hell to catch when they get away," he grins. One night, to find an elusive female, he had to remove all the paneling from one wall.

Fannin, however, has more worries than his precious hamsters.

"I'm no young man anymore," he says. "Thirty-seven is not 25." That is another reality he understands – that and where he'll continue to work – in the shop.

"They got me hooked," he says. "I got into credit and I can't get out. The more I want, the more I borrow and you just can't get out. And they know it. They do it to you. Hell, I know it. They got me and I'm hooked and I know it. I'm gone."

He is gone from Catlettsburg and simple boyhood days of tossing rocks in quiet ponds and swinging through Kentucky hollers on vines draped from trees; gone from the specter of life in southern coal mines to the stark realities of the industrial North; gone from a happy level of poverty to higher wages he earns but never sees, Fannin is hooked to the confused American dream.

Junior Fannin finds himself living in a place that isn't home, grown up in a world unlike the one that spawned and nurtured him, watching a television that doesn't work, trying to spell Catlettsburg.

C-a-t-l-e-t-t-s-b-u-r-g.

In Pennsylvania they play for keeps

It wasn't as if Eddie Holmes' mother didn't try to do a good job raising him. It was just that times were basically hard.

"She brought us up the best she could. I didn't hang in the street or anything like that," said Holmes, 36.

A native of Pittsburgh, Holmes is serving a life sentence for first-degree murder in the State Correctional Institute in Dallas.

His father divorced his mother, leaving Holmes and his brothers and sisters in a difficult position.

"My mom worked real hard, but we didn't have a lot of money," Holmes said.

Holmes dropped out of high school in his senior year, joined the Navy, worked on jet engines in a helicopter squadron and received an honorable discharge. After the service, he tried to enroll in school to continue his mechanical training but was unable to find his way into a class.

"It was overcrowded."

So Holmes took a job driving a taxi. And Holmes began hustling cocaine.

"There were a lot of problems. You did what you had to do. I had to take to the streets to make a living," he said. "The lure of the fast buck got me."

He was 25 years old. And his days of freedom were fading fast.

"The police were constantly harassing me, trying to find some way to bust me."

An armed robbery charge didn't stick. Then there was a fatal shooting following an aborted cocaine deal. Holmes was charged and ultimately convicted of first-degree murder.

"I wasn't even involved, but whether I was guilty or innocent had no bearing," he said. "If they want you, they get you. Someone had to be arrested. They must clear the books. All they want are convictions."

In Holmes' case, a witness to the fatal shooting implicated him.

"The guy was a junkie," Holmes said. "He turned state's evidence against me. At the time he was facing 11 indictments. He'd pled guilty to all of them. After he testified against me, they let him off. He went home and I came here."

On December 12, 1975, Holmes was convicted in Allegheny County of first-degree murder. He is still attempting to appeal the verdict, claiming that his court-appointed attorney provided inadequate assistance. The appeal process has been slow and discouraging. It has not been helped by the fact Holmes and his family in Pittsburgh has very little money to pay for attorneys. Yet the appeals process is all Holmes has.

"There's only three ways for a lifer to get out of jail in this state," he said. "The courts, the fence or the box."

Lifers seeking to get out of prison in Pennsylvania have one other option: seeking to have their sentences commuted by the governor. To gain commutation, however, a prisoner must first admit his guilt. Holmes said he isn't ready to take that path.

"I'm not atypical," Holmes said. "Very seldom will you find a guy in here who will say he did it. After all, in a homicide only two people know what happened and only one of them walked away. You never know about the exact circumstances. Was someone provoked? Did the guy jump on him? Was it self-defense? You rarely get the answers to these kinds of questions."

Guilty or innocent, Holmes said he is obsessed with the idea of getting out of prison.

"I do want out," he said. "I might ultimately go the commutation route. You want me to say I did it to get out, fine. If not, I'll just keep fighting the way I've been fighting. I do know if they'd give me that shot they'd never see me in here again. There's no maybe about it because I know what this place is about and I'm not coming back here."

More and more Pennsylvania residents are learning what jail is about. There are more killers serving life sentences for murder in the state than ever before. And in Pennsylvania, a life sentence usually means just that.

"You never stop trying with your case but you're constantly hitting snags," said Samuel Clark, an inmate serving a life sentence in the Dallas prison.

"More times than not you're turned down. The system is structured so that our appeals don't get a true hearing."

In 1983, only three of the 1,195 inmates sentenced to life imprisonment for first- degree murder were released from Pennsylvania state prisons.

"Some people in my family thought when I was sentenced to life that I'd be getting out in around 10 years or so," Clark said. "They didn't understand that 'life' in Pennsylvania means what it says."

So far, Clark has served seven years in prison.

In 1972, those serving life sentences in the state numbered 402; by 1983 the number had increased to 1,420, a rise of 167 percent. More than half of them are from Philadelphia. Their average age is 34. Thirty of them are 60 or older.

The statistics are available in large numbers. But the story they tell doesn't completely cover the subject, according to the lifers themselves.

*   *   *

"The public thinks we're some kind of monsters," Eddie Holmes said. "It's not so. We're not the ogres society believes we are. The reason people think the way they do about us is because of the media, which only shows one side. There are two sides to every story. All we want to do is show the public that we are not the inhuman creatures they make us out to be. All we want is what anybody else would want; a second chance."

"Most lifers have themselves under control. Our main motive and drive is to get released. Every state we go through is just another stage of hope. Very few lifers are able to go through the court system and get released. You either die or you get communication. Hope is all we function on and with commutation there's very little hope at the moment."

*   *   *

Eddie Holmes and Samuel Clark are members of the executive board of the L.I.F.E. Association (the initials stand for Life Isn't For Ever) at the Dallas prison. They are but two of the 227 lifers in the prison, a 25-year-old institution with a capacity for 940 inmates. The current prison population is 1,610.

"I feel basically the lifer is an inmate who has a made a one-time mistake and not someone who is a hardened criminal," said Jay Miller, director of activities at the Dallas prison and an advocate of the lifers club.

"Many times they come from middle-class homes. They're just like you and me. In 10 years of dealing with lifers I've had very little problems with them. There are certain lifers who should be locked up for life and a day and there are others who deserve something better. Generally, they're people who acted out of emotions and they're deserving of consideration."

"Reporters aren't exactly beating down our doors to talk to them but they do have a story to tell. These are human beings. These are men. They made mistakes. Some mistakes are bigger than others."

Paul Ware, 39, a lifer at Dallas from Philadelphia for the 12 years since he was convicted of first-degree murder, said the average lifer understands the significance of his wrongdoing.

"We can see society's side of the coin," he said. "We grieve for our misunderstandings. All we want is a chance to prove ourselves. At this point, though, it's hard to keep the faith."

The lack of optimism expressed by lifers is based on hard facts.

From January, 1979 through December, 1983, the five-man Board of Pardons appointed by Gov. Dick Thornburgh received 289 applications for commutation, 266 of which were heard. The board recommended 50 of the appeals; only four were granted.

As a matter of contrast, former Gov. Milton Shapp commuted a total of 254 life sentences in the eight years he was in office, 45 percent of the cases that came before him.

In 1976, prison officials let out 23 convicted first- degree murderers and in 1978 they freed 27. The 1978 figure is nine times as many lifers as were released in 1983.

David Bayne, secretary of the Pennsylvania Board of Pardons, said life prisoners who are granted freedom are no longer released immediately from state prisons.

"It used to be that all lifers granted clemency had their sentences commuted to time served and they were given immediate parole," Bayne said.

"But in the mid-1970s, the pardons board changed its methods of commuting life sentences. Now, no lifers go out on time served. They are given a post-dated minimum."

If the pardons board believes an inmate who has served a portion of his sentence is no longer a threat to the community, the board may commute his sentence and give him a parole date two years from the present time.

If the inmate continues to behave and show progress, he will be paroled. During the two years between the pardon boards' commutation and the parole date, the inmate participates in pre-release programs such as furloughs and will be transferred from a walled prison to a community service center near his hometown.

*   *   *

'Life…electric word, means forever…and that's a mighty long time.'

-   Prince, songwriter

 Eddie Holmes will have served 10 years in prison as of

May. He has completed his high school education and

earned 75 college credits toward a bachelors degree in

communications.

Holmes worked an eight-hour day sewing covers in the prison mattress shop. He earns 37 cents an hour, the top hourly wage at Chase. During his leisure time he officiates basketball games and serves as external vice-president of the L.I.F.E. Association.

Holmes said he manages to get by in jail, if only in a marginal sense. He says he tried to avoid conflicts in the prison, with an emphasis on staying away from dope dealers and "chasing boys." Everyday he feels he must prove himself, both to himself and to the prison authorities.

"It's very tough," he said. "I've lost my property and my job, I've been held up to public ridicule and ostracized by society. I'm the lowest of the low. It's a hell of a thing. Everyday I say to myself, 'Well, maybe tomorrow.'

"If and when I get out of here the first thing I'm going to do is get a see-through lunch box so everyone will know I'm working," he said.

Holmes said he would like to continue his education and get a job that would allow him to work with children and perhaps help them avoid prison.

Holmes deliberated for only a moment when asked what he would say to a citizen on the street who would question his right to leave prison after being convicted of murder.

"I'd ask them if they had any morals," he said. "I'd ask them if they'd ever made any mistakes in their life and if they had, I'd ask them if they believed they deserved a second chance. If you take away the second chance, you take away society. No one is perfect. That's why even the smartest man needs pencils with erasers."

Kamerer Disappearance: Officials withhold aid

(Editor's Note: It's been almost six months since Bill and Patty Kamerer disappeared. Their boat, the Kalia III, was discovered off Pipe Cay in the Bahamas in early August. Early reports that a body was found on the attached dinghy were denied – then later acknowledged – by Bahamian authorities investigating the case.

Some say the Kamerers were unwilling victims of area drug racketeers. Many, like the Bahamian officials charged with investigating the case, say the real reason behind their disappearance might never be known. At least three people – Bill Kamerer's son, William, of Rochester; State Sen. Harry Yourell of Illinois; and the Kamerer's best friend, Skip Nichols of Fort Myers – aren't satisfied with the investigation. They're especially determined that whatever happened to the Kamerers doesn't befall any future visitors to the area.

Oakland Press reporter Trout Pomeroy spent nearly three weeks in Florida with Nichols and the young Kamerer. This is the first of three articles on their story.)

FORT MYERS BEACH, Fla. – Skip Nichols glances at a wall calendar that sits in a dusty pose on a shelf behind him in the hold of his sailboat.

Though it's late December, the calendar is still set on the month of August – when the news of the disappearance of Bill and Patty Kamerer in Fort Myers spread across the world.

For Nichols, a 34-year-old marina operator, life has stood still since August, when Kamerer, his best friend, was apparently murdered by pirates or drug smugglers in the Bahama Islands.

It is a balmy evening in late December. Talking to a visitor, Nichols advances a serious sense of purpose.

His 41-foot sailboat lies moored off a pier behind an imposing aluminum warehouse that is called the Fish Tail Marina.

Darkness prevails. His working day is through. Nichols has showered. A full beard graces his suntanned face. A few bottles of beer and a stack of scrapbooks sit on a table between the marina operator and his guest.

Nichols met Kamerer in the mid-1970s through a sailing club both men belonged to, the Caloosahatchee Marching and Chowder Society. The club is names after the Caloosahatchee River, a murky-blue body of water that flows past Fort Myers into the Gulf of Mexico.

The river helps make Fort Myers the unique city it is, an urban center, which manages to be not only a high-density boating center and a fast-growing retirement area, but also a southern metropolis that maintains a basically commercial orientation.

Nichols operates the Fish Tail Marina at Fort Myers Beach – a stretch of white-sanded shores, condominiums, hotels and boating-related commerce that extends across fingers of islands and bridges west of downtown Fort Myers.

Bill Kamerer and his wife Patty moved to Fort Myers Beach five years ago. The Nichols and Kamerers sailed and raced together. Both had 41-foot sailboats. They became best friends.

"Bill was a dynamic sailor," Nichols remembers. "He's the one who really taught me how to handle a boat.

"He knew a lot not only about the pleasure of sailing," Nichols said. "He knew how to be proficient, how to sail to your maximum potential."

Kamerer, Nichols said, "was like a man 50, going on 30." Their friendship was strong.

"We complemented each other," Nichols said, "because I'm like 34, going on 50. We really enjoyed each other's company."

Nichols spent nearly four years helping the Kamerers construct their dreamboat, the Kalia III. After wishing the couple well as they embarked upon a long awaited five-month cruise, Nichols and his wife kept in touch with Bill and Patty by radio, telephone and letters.

In early summer, after the Kamerers had participated with some success in a five-race series of regattas, the Nichols sailed to the Bahamas where the couples met up for another two weeks of sailing.

Among the popular areas they visited was Marsh Harbor, a popular rendezvous point for sailors. On July 21, the Nichols said goodbye to the Kamerers over their boat radios and sailed back to Fort Myers.

It was to be their last communication.

*   *   *

Early on the morning of Aug. 2, Nichols received a phone call from another of Kamerer's closest friends, Ellen Springer of Fort Myers. She told Nichols that the U.S. State Department had just contacted the Kamerer's son William Jr., with news of the discovery of the abandoned Kalia.

A self-described "aggressive person," Nichols leapt to action.

"Having just been with them, I decided I had to find out what was going on," Nichols said.

"Bill was my best friend," he said. "You just don't walk away from those kind of things."

*   *   *

With the discovery of their abandoned sailboat last summer in the Bahama Islands, what had begun as an adventure for Bill and Patty Kamerer apparently came to a tragic end. But, in the wake of their disappearance, a new adventure had also begun.

•   It started when Harry Yourell of Illinois, who was in the Bahamas on a sailing adventure of his own at the time with his son Pete, decided to take out his cameras and record what he had found at Pipe Cay when he discovered the Kamerer's abandoned sailboat, the Kalia III.

•   And it was most significantly advanced when Nichols caught wind of Yourell's discovery and pledged to join forces with the legislator in trying to find answers to the mysterious apparent double murder of the Kamerers.

Before the summer was over, Yourell's grisly photos of the Kalia III and dinghy had run on the front pages of newspapers across the country. And seven minutes of 16 millimeter movie film of the abandoned Kalia and the dinghy – also shot by Yourell – were seen on a nationally broadcast morning news television program.

From the beginning, Nichols says his experience in dealing with the matter has been "frustrating and aggravating."

After hearing from the Springers, Nichols learned that a pilot from a private Fort Lauderdale aviation company had flown into Staniel Key at the time the abandoned Kalia was found and had photographed the boat and dinghy from the air.

The pilot confirmed he had "seen something" in the dinghy. And the pilot wasn't alone in his assessment. The Bahamian government, in fact, also confirmed that a body had been spotted hanging out of the dinghy by their own investigators.

Unfortunately, Nichols subsequently learned, those investigators were less than adequately prepared and somewhat less-than willing to conduct an immediate investigation of what they found.

For Nichols though, as well as for a number of Kamerer's other friends in the Fort Myer boating community, an active investigation – one that continues to this day – began in earnest.

"We knew after the first time we flew over their boat and saw that there wasn't anything more we could do for Bill and Patty," said Nichols, a short, blonde-haired man with the intense stare of a superb linebacker.

"Obviously, the only thing left to do was to try and get the boat back here to Fort Myers and then, after that, to just continue to make the public and the boating community aware of the fact that there are many potential problems involved with sailing in the Bahamas. "People who chose to take that vacation route -- and it is a beautiful place to go – will have to know that they will have to take a number of precautions if they're actually bold enough to want to go over there.

"That's all that's left now. We've lost Patty and Bill, but what we can't lose sight of is that we don't want what happened to them to happen to anyone else down there."

What actually happened to Bill and Patty Kamerer remains of some official conjecture. Yourell's photographs assure that. They show a body – one that closely resembles Kamerer's – in a dinghy.

The photos are not legally binding with respect to the Kamerer inquiry. The Bahamian government never recovered the body from the dinghy and has yet to decide whether the Kamerers were officially murdered or are, in fact, missing persons.

Nichols has been immersed in the controversy surrounding the failure of the Bahamians to secure the body.

Of major complications, he said, the Bahamians claimed they arrived at Pipe Cay late in the evening, without a mortician or even a body-bag in which to secure the body that had been reported to be hanging from the dinghy.

Observers at the scene, including Nichols, refute this version, saying the officials did in fact have a body bag.

Because it was getting dark and the authorities were reluctant to tow the boat and dinghy into Staniel Key due to odors emanating from the body in the dinghy, Nichols said the Bahamians decided to leave the scene intact until the following morning.

By the following morning, the body was missing. Officials then towed the Kalia to a government port facility in Nassau.

By August 5, both Nichols and Bill Kamerer Jr., 27, had arrived in the Bahamas to try to find out more about the disappearance of the couple. "We wanted to know what happened," Nichols said.

Bahamian officials took the men to Pipe Cay, where Nichols found what he later called, "a beautiful little anchorage."

The next day, in Nassau, Nichols found that the chief Bahamian investigator in the case had not yet been to examine the Kalia.

"We were really teed-off by things like that," he said. "We just couldn't believe how poorly they were handling the situation. They didn't know what to look for. I think we were more informed than they were. I guess it's just a different country and they do things as they want to."

Nichols and another Fort Myers sailor, Jim Stimson, examined the Kalia themselves. The men discovered that an apparent shotgun blast had left pellet marks on the starboard stern of the boat. The pellet marks and the damage of the Kalia's exterior-mounted navigational log was the only tangible damage Nichols and Stimson could see.

"It hadn't blown a hole in it," Nichols said. "It just looked like little BB shots had (been fired at) the boat's surface."

Meanwhile, an official Bahamian investigator of the matter determined that there was "nary a bullet mark or hole" on the boat. Nevertheless, Nichols now speculates that a second shotgun blast may have killed his friend Kamerer.

After visiting the Kalia at its government mooring in Nassau, Nichols and Stimson returned to Fort Myers and Bill Kamerer Jr., to Rochester.

"There didn't seem to be anything else we could do (there) at that point," Nichols explained.

Back in Fort Myers, however, Nichols continued his personal investigation. "I was pretty much resigned to the fact that the body on that dinghy was Bill," he said, "even though I still had a small inkling of hope he might be alive."

But his hopes were met with frustration.

"Nobody could help," Nichols said. "The State Department, local politicians, the Coast Guard, the FBI, none of them cared. The U.S. has absolutely no jurisdiction over there. It's just like the situation in Iran now…the U.S. couldn't just march in and take over the situation. It was just a fact of life. We couldn't do anything."

In Rochester, Bill Kamerer, Jr. said, "The State Department has done nothing except to say that they can do nothing. My parents may have been slaughtered by pirates, picked off like moving targets on the open sea."

For a month, Skip Nichols in Florida and Bill Kamerer, Jr. in Rochester both felt as if they were in limbo. Then, in late August, Yourell's photographs were published, first in Ft. Lauderdale and subsequently around the world. And things began to stir.

Yourell told Nichols he would do everything he could to keep the investigation alive. And determined to proceed with his own investigation of the matter, Nichols arranged for photographs of the Kamerers to be distributed among those who might have more information leading up to the couple's mysterious disappearance.

A reward fund was also established.

Through his repeated appearances on local news broadcasts, others in the south Florida boating community learned of Nichols' efforts. Many wrote to the young marina operator, encouraging him to continue his search for further information.

"If you don't stay with the investigation, people will forget and the case will never be solved," one correspondent argued to Nichols. So Nichols persists.

His efforts bore fruit last fall when two separate parties of boaters who had been in the area of Pipe Cay at the time of the Kamerer's disappearance confirmed to Nichols that they had each observed motor boats circling the Kalia in the days preceding Yourell's discovery of the abandoned boat.

The motor boats, the observers reported, were of a variety known as "cigarette-type" boats, a reference describing the narrow size of high-speed type boats.

All the witnesses told Nichols that they felt there was a suspicious nature of activity surrounding the motor boats and the Kalia.

Nichols' pursuit of additional information continues. Report released on missing pair

The case of William and Patty Kamerer, the former Oakland County couple who are missing from their abandoned sailboat in waters off a quiet key in the Bahama Islands in July, appears to be officially closed.

Last week, Bahamian officials released a report on the incident.

The report, which offers no specific conclusions, is expected to be the final official act in connection with the three-month investigation.

"That's probably going to be the last of it, unless they make an arrest or find the two of them on some island, neither of which will probably happen," said a Miami newsman.

"They're (the Bahamians) not giving any explanation," a British news source in Nassau told the Oakland Press. "They play with words and don't cooperate very much."

Governmental officials on the Atlantic island have been accused of a cover-up. They have denied such accusations.

The final report, though, raises at least one significant question.

After the Kamerer's 41-foot sailboat, the Kalia III, was discovered adrift and abandoned in late July by another American tourist who was sailing in the same waters, reports circulated that a body had been attached to a small dinghy being towered by the Kamerers' boat.

Photos of the alleged body ran in newspapers across the country, yet the Bahamians continued to deny they found such a body when they first inspected the abandoned craft.

However, in last week's report, the government admitted a body had been attached to the dinghy.

The report details events that followed the July 31 discovery of the boat. It explains that government officials failed to initially secure the controversial body because of "its odor" and because an airplane could not be immediately secured to dispatch the body to an autopsy center.

The officials discovered the body had disappeared when they returned to the Kalia III. In any event, the report does not account for the discrepancy it creates with original official accounts. Disappearance has sailors wary

Eighteen months after a Michigan couple disappeared while sailing in a remote area off the Bahama Islands, authorities are no closer to solving the mystery than they were the day when the bullet-ridden sailboat was found.

Although the investigation into the disappearance and probable death of William and Patty Kamerer has faded from the headlines, the ramifications of the incident remain a prominent factor within the South Atlantic sailing community.

Jane Baumann, a reporter who covered the Kamerer incident for the St. Petersburg Evening Times Independent, now says she feels the disappearance of the Fort Myers, Fla., couple had an important effect on "the cruising industry" because the wide publicity the incident received.

"After this Kamerer thing happened, anyone having anything to do with tourism in the Bahamas was trying like mad to whitewash and play down the incident," she said.

"But the people in the local boating community around here knew what was happening. In fact, they'd already started to change their attitudes on the subject."

William Kamerer and his wife, Patty, disappeared on the last day of July in 1980. Another visiting American sailor, Henry Yourell of Oak Park, Ill., discovered the Kamerer's bullet-ridden 41-foot sailboat, the Kalia III, near Pipe Cay in the Exumas on Aug. 1.

Yourell, an Illinois state legislator, said there was no one aboard Kalia III when he and his son discovered the boat; but Yourell claimed he and his son saw a man's body hanging over the side of a dinghy that was attached by a rope to the abandoned boat.

To substantiate his discovery, Yourell produced a series of astonishing photographs of the scene he and his son had discovered. A wave of interest followed.

Kamerer's son, William Jr., who lives in the Rochester area, cooperated with the media by sharing the story of his effort to work with Bahamian authorities to investigate the crime.

The investigation, unfortunately, bore no significant results.

The resulting attitude change, Ms. Baumann said, showed up as individuals planning to cruise to the Bahamas began traveling in groups.

And they began carrying more arms.

"You could tell that it was just after that (the Kamerer incident) happened, that the sporting goods stores down here started specializing more and more in stainless steel guns, or rust-free guns, for boaters. I think they're sort of a big item now."

In addition to traveling in groups and carrying arms, Ms. Baumann said boaters visiting the Bahamas now have a greater tendency to anchor at night in groups, rather than seeking out quiet moorings, as the Kamerers apparently had done.

"People don't go just anywhere like they once did," she said. "They're a lot more conscious of the things that can happen over there."

In Fort Myers Beach, where the Kamerers lived, their former best friend, Skip Nichols, agreed with Ms. Baumann's theory.

"I think this particular incident created enough notoriety to increase people's awareness and make all sailors down here more group-oriented in their planning," Nichols, a marina operator, said.

"Everyone travels in groups now, anchors together in groups, and pretty much stays together, for obvious reasons of safety and security."

The Kamerer incident, Nichols said, may have been the key to this turnaround in thinking.

"I personally feel what it (the incident) did was open people's eyes to the true situation over there. It made them wake up a little and say, 'Wow, even paradise has problems, just like New York City.'"

Sailors aren't necessarily staying away from the Bahamas because of what happened to the Kamerers, Nichols said. But they are being more careful.

"If someone was shot and killed say, at Disney World, I don't think that would mean people would stop going there," he said.

"The same is true in the Bahamas. It's still an attraction. And people are still going there. But they're going there with a different awareness of what could happen to them then they had before." Kamerer Case: 'Maybe something will get done'

FORT MEYERS BEACH, Fla. – Charging the U.S. State Department with "ignoring a grisly case of piracy and bloodshed," Illinois state legislator Harry Yourell in August demanded that an investigation be conducted into the facts surrounding the disappearance of Bill and Patty Kamerer.

It was Yourell who a month earlier had happened upon the Kamerer's abandoned sailboat.

Encouraged by other boaters who wrote him, many saying they had been attacked by pirates in the Bahamas, Yourell also said he would launch a newspaper ad campaign to warn boaters of what he said were dangers posed by drug traffickers in the islands.

Yourell has not begun the ad campaign, but still feels it will be the most effective step he can take. He has learned that the problem is much larger than the killing of two innocent people.

Yourell said that many sailors are now avoiding waters surrounding the Bahamas in favor of sailing in other areas such as the Virgin Islands.

Much of the concern stems from the Bahamian government's apparent lax stand towards incidents like the Kamerer disappearance and the drug pirates that roam the waters around the Bahamas.

Bahamian government officials, who have jurisdiction over the Kamerer case, say they have no leads.

"Unless they happen to come across some new evidence, which is about as likely as a major snowfall happening down here, the case is closed," said a Florida reporter familiar with the Kamerer story. "The only way anything will ever happen now will be if someone involved comes forward and confesses, for whatever reason. But over on the islands, that would be pretty unlikely because of the secrecy and the way the people are all related to each other. But then again, the Bahamians might surprise us."

While the Bahamian government has apparently stalled in its investigation of the matter, the search for clues into the disappearance of the Kamerers continues.

Illinois state legislator Harry Yourell continues to push from his end. And Fort Myers marina operator Skip Nichols is pursuing the matter in Florida with equal determination.

Early in September, another encouraging development began in Washington, D.C., when a congressional committee began hearings into the disappearance of the Kamerers.

Committee members indicated they planned to use their investigation as a vehicle with which to stage a larger probe of hijacking, piracy and drug running in the Caribbean.

The investigation is necessary, said Rep. Lester Wolff, D-N.Y., because luxury boats like the Kamerer's are vulnerable to pirates.

"Many of these large luxury boats and smaller cigarettes (sleek, high-powered speedboats) are eyed by traffickers as convenient means of transportation, like a stolen car," said Wolff, who is chairman of the U.S. Select Committee on Narcotics Abuse and Control.

"The owners and passengers, unfortunately, are minor characters to these characters and they get wasted."

In Rochester, Bill Kamerer Jr. said he was encouraged by news of the congressional investigation into the disappearance of his father.

"You know, I thought I was going crazy," he said from his home on a quiet residential street south of Rochester.

"We couldn't get anybody interested and we couldn't get any straight answers about what happened down there. Now maybe someone will get something done."

In late August, the congressional representative from the Fort Myers area, U.S. Rep. L.A. Bafalis, R-Fla., sent a letter to Secretary of State Edmund Muskie saying that the Kamerer case "has been handled with gross inefficiency by both the Bahamian government and by our State Department."

In Illinois, Yourell said he plans to go to Washington in January after the new Congress has been installed to call for a continuation of the investigation into the Kamerer matter.

"I understand that all the old top brass in the State Department will be gone by then so maybe we'll get some action," Yourell said.

Until then, Yourell said he remains frustrated in his efforts to pursue the Kamerer case.

"What burns me more than anything is that I've made all this information available to the State Department and they're really not concerned. I think there must be a lot of American interest in the tourism business in the Bahamas and the State Department has been told not to rock the boat. There's millions of American dollars invested in the area…that's all I can conclude.

"You've got to realize that tourism is the No. 1 industry in the Bahamas, employing three out of every four people down there," he said in a recent telephone interview.

"I hate to cause harm to those working in the tourism industry. But I think the Bahamian government has to be made aware there is grave concern among people in this country regarding the lack of safety down there."

Thomas Newcomer of the State Department's Overseas Citizens Services division said in August that the State Department is planning no investigation.

"Action in this case isn't up to us. It's up to the Bahamian government," Newcomer said. "The incident happened in the Bahamian waters and we have no jurisdiction there. The only thing we can do is report what they (the Bahamians) tell us and urge them to act more quickly."

Responding to Yourell and other critics, Bahamian government officials have repeatedly said that the drug trafficking phenomenon currently plaguing the Bahamas is an American problem that should be fought with American tax dollars.

"The invasion comes from her shores and is conducted by her citizens," Bahamian Prime Minister Lynden Pindling said at a late September news conference in Washington, D.C. "It is up to the United States to do something positive to control the invasion and stop it before it completely destroys the Bahamas."

The primes minister called for the U.S. to either lend or give the government $25 million worth of boats, aircraft and communications equipment to help his government fight "the armed invasion of drug criminals from the north."

At the same press conference, Robert Feldcamp, a public affairs officer for the Drug Enforcement Agency (DEA), said the single most important step the Bahamians can take is to sign a treaty with the Unites States that would provide for the exchange of criminal and financial information among law enforcement agencies in two countries.

With a congressional investigation still in process, the U.S. State Department and the DEA on alert and the Bahamian prime minister finally speaking out on the matter, it appears the disappearance of William and Patty Kamerer may be turning out to be something more than just "one more isolated incident" as the Bahamians originally claimed.

As Bill Kamerer's 85-year-old mother, Mabel Kamerer of Royal Oak said the week after her son's disappearance, "Think of it, this story is going out all over the world. I'm convinced God must have picked Billy for this so everybody would know there was a nest of murderers over there in the Bahamas. I think this all might have happened to blow this dope business thing up. One little boat and it's heard all over the world. It's fantastic to think of the coverage it's gotten."

Kamerer's son drained over disappearance

ROCHESTER – Five months after the late-July disappearance of his father and step-mother from their 41- foot sailboat in the waters off an isolated island in the Bahamas, Bill Kamerer Jr., has been left exhausted, both verbally and emotionally.

"I'm just about talked out," the dark-haired, 27-year- old auto mechanic told a reporter who visited his home on a late December night.

Kamerer made no effort to smile as he nestled his large frame into a corner chair in the living room of his two- story frame house at the end of a long, unpaved road in an old, wooden subdivision south of Rochester.

His wife, Cindy, and the family's German shepherd nearby, Kamerer pointed to a color photograph of smiling Bill and Patty Kamerer. The picture, taken on an earlier vacation trip, sat alone in a gold-colored frame atop a nearby book case.

"At first, I didn't want to upset the apple cart," he said. "I went along with what the Bahamian were telling me. It seemed they were taking the proper steps."

After a month, however, Kamerer began to suspect the investigation was going nowhere. And contradictions from the Bahamain government, he said, made it difficult to get a clear idea of what may have happened to his father in the blue waters of Pipe Cay.

"As far as I'm concerned, they conned me," he said.

The Bahamians originally denied spotting a body hanging from a dinghy behind Kamerer's father's boat, the Kalia III. The Bahamians later admitted to having seen the body.

And there were other discrepancies.

When the younger Kamerer inspected the boat in Nassau in December, he claims it was in the same condition as when it had been found in late July.

"I don't know how they (Bahamian authorities) could have examined it," he said. "Everything's been so contradictory."

Nevertheless, Kamerer has come up with his own theory of what may have happened.

"It's always been my belief that what happened was just simple robbery. It was too sloppy for drug people."

Drug traffickers, Kamerer theorized, would not have left the Kalia "flopping about" as the boat was when Illinois legislator Harry Yourell and his son discovered it. Instead, Kamerer said, they would have towed the Kalia the short distance out to sea and sunk it.

Whether at the hands of bandits or drug dealers, Bill Kamerer Jr. knows his father met his death at Pipe Cay.

"It would have been easier to accept if they had disappeared under normal conditions at sea – in a storm or something," Kamerer said. "In the boating community, they expect things like that to happen. But the violent part is what gets me. It's like he was taken from us right off my front porch here and shot down."

"We still would have had a lot of time to spend together ahead of us. I'm glad we were friends, but all I can think about was the time we still had."

The passing time, he said, has allowed Kamerer and his 26-year-old brother Jim, of Royal Oak, to begin living almost normal lives again.

For the boy's grandmother, however – 85-year-old Mabel Kamerer of Royal Oak – the uncertainty and loss has not been easy.

"That's the only real tough spot now," Kamerer said. "Grandma still hasn't given up hope that he still might be alive. I hate to think of the day it finally comes crashing down on her."

When his father's birthday came and went with no phone call, Kamerer said his grandmother, a widow, came closer to accepting the possibility that he may not be alive. When Christmas came and went with no phone call, that knowledge sank in even further.

"Sometimes she's real good and sometimes you just don't know," he said.

In any event, Kamerer's grandmother does not want the Kalia sold.

But that's not an immediate issue. Until a Florida probate court determines the boat's future, the Kalia will remain in the custody of Skip Nichols in Fort

Meyers. Before making a determination, the probate court will review the Bahamian government's final findings.

"It could drag on for quite a while," said Kamerer.

Kamerer stood up, signaling an end to the conversation.

"Nobody will be able to say I didn't say my side on the thing now," he said. "I guess I don't mind talking about it, if it will help keep the investigation going. I'd still like to know what happened."

'Lvis' reached out to all his fans

Larry Berby understands the ongoing Elvis craze.

"When he died, "Berby, a 37-year-old General Motors technician from Highland Township says, "people were still looking for more. They just didn't want to believe he was dead."

Like Berby, an estimated 1,500 Elvis-imitators haven't missed the point.

At least 60 of them work their curious craft in Michigan, including 26-year-old Cliff Shelton, now in the process of changing his first name to "Lvis."

Shelton is also auditioning for the lead role in a Presley film tribute that will be called, "The King of Rock & Roll," currently being cast in New York City.

"We're looking for a complete unknown and he's under consideration," Robert Harris, an assistant producer with Diamond Films says.

Harris says that Shelton is one of four finalists who were selected from the nearly 200 Elvis look-alikes responding to the film company's first of what Harris says will be four rounds of auditions for the Presley part.

Diamond officials told Shelton the casting decision would be made by March 1.

Shelton – whose popular Elvis act packed the Wishing Well Lounge in Highland Township last week with a happy variety of analytic-types like Larry Berby – bears remarkable resemblance to the late Presley.

From the breadth of his full-blown sideburns, that cascade down his puffy cheeks like broad strips of carpeting, to the sulking southern drawl and swaggered swivel of his hips, Lvis apes Elvis, the perfect ringer of the fundamental singer.

"He touches a lot of people," Shelton's publicist, Quentin Lutes, says.

More than one thousand of them, in fact, belong to Shelton's fan club.

"People are what it's all about for him," Lutes says. "All he wants to do is reach out and make them happy, through Elvis' music, even though he really doesn't think he's Elvis."

Shelton has successfully parlayed this fortuitous affinity for eight years, traversing the thin line between his own personality and Presley's in a variety of Detroit- area clubs, including, on the July night in 1977 when Presley died, the Redwood Lounge in Livonia.

His wife Sandy had been listening to the radio while working in the front yard that summer afternoon when the tragic news came from Tennessee. "I went inside and told Cliff he'd better sit down," she recalls.

'I didn't want to work that night," Shelton says.

Nevertheless, the show went on.

"When Elvis died, the whole world cried," Sandy, his wife and mother of his four children says. "Lvis tells me this all the time." Last summer they went to Memphis on the anniversary of Presley's death, visiting Graceland – the late singer's mansion – and most of the Elvis memorabilia stores flourishing in that city. "We bought everything we could get our hand on," Shelton claims.

Born in North Carolina and raised in Detroit, Shelton attended school through junior high before beginning his musical career. His father taught him to play guitar when he was seven and by his twelfth birthday, he was playing along with the first of his Elvis records.

Fourteen years later, the obsession continues. "I know most of his songs and have seen all his movies about 12 times each," Shelton says.

With only occasional lapses, Shelton's voice confirms the fact, smacking the essential from the lowest of his growls to his most resonant tenor, while the dynamics of his live performance extend the similarity even further.

After his four-piece band has warmed the audience, the lights go down and the show starts. With the band playing the prelude to the film, "2001 – A Space Odyssey" – with much transcedent implication – off-stage technicians ring bells, sound sirens and flash spotlights about the room until Shelton appears, replete with overstated yet standard Presley-style garb and not-to-be-played yet de rigeur guitar.

With women screaming, with busboys scurrying about cleaning ashtrays, Shelton writhes and wiggles his way through famous Presley songs like, "C.C. Rider, "Teddy Bear," and "Don't Be Cruel," wading into the crowd at times and prefacing each selection with the stock show-biz phrase, "This one goes something like this…"

The effect is impressive. While Shelton sings "Fools Rush In," women rush the stage, grabbing for one of the ten scarfs (that cost $2 each) that he systematically surrenders to the audience each night. Over the years they've gouged his chest, poked fingers in his eyes and actually knocked the poor guy off his feet on occasion.

Four women came at once, one legendary night, trying for the same scarf. Unfortunately, they knocked him in the chops with his microphone, necessitating 13 stitches.

Mouth intact, Shelton will be performing in Milford during March at the La-Catina Lounge, unless, of course, the boys at Diamond Films in New York decide otherwise.

May you stay forever young, Bob Dylan

Paradise! Sacrifice! Mortality! Reality! Bob Dylan reels off the thoughts – from his new song, "No Time to Think" – with the fervor of the world's holiest rolling gospel preacher. Which, within the terms of popular culture today, is essentially what he has become.

Thirty-six-year-old Bob Dylan says that he started writing songs before he could walk. Long after he is gone, the best of them will live, perhaps on a level with the work of William Shakespeare.

Both men led mystic lives, elusively clouded in the mystery. Both had tremendous memories and were the central artists of their day. But only Dylan is coming to Detroit's Olympia Stadium on Oct. 13.

"I'm a poet, too," Dylan – who had three successful record albums out at the time – told Carl Sandburg, who had never heard of him, in 1964.

A week later, in New Orleans, Dylan borrowed a young street singer's guitar and strummed a few tunes. "Man," the kid exclaimed. "You sound just like Bob Dylan."

Bob's face was impassive. "Saw Dylan once," he said. "A place in the Village. He's all right, I guess." Bob Dylan, as in Dylan Thomas, Dylan Thomas, as in poet extraordinaire.

In Minnesota, in the late 1950s, with locusts singing in the fields outside his graduation ceremony at Hibbing High School, Robert Zimmerman, the frail son of a Jewish appliance store owner, began his transformation into Bob Dylan, the strong father of popular music.

Before he had finished his freshman year at the University of Minnesota, Zimmerman-Dylan advanced the metamorphosis significantly, splitting for New York City, and, once there, quickly coming to dominate the folk music scene.

Dylan voiced the passions and hitherto ineffable aggrievements of his generation. As singer Joan Baez said, "Bobby Dylan says what a lot of people my age feel but cannot say."

Other folk singers had groped for vestiges of tradition and authenticity in anonymous old ballads about Lord- Somebody-or-other and roses growing out of stones. Then Dylan came along, with his own compositions about current topics, with lyrics that flowed forth with direct contemporary protest. He changed the scene.

His songs challenged the consciousness of those that heard them, from 1961, when his first recording, "Bob Dylan" was released, until now, with his 18th album, "Street Legal."

"Mercury rules you and destiny fools you," he sings to his muse and he sings to the world, in "Street Legal," 18 albums closer to immortality. With fire and pertinence, Dylan remains, in 1978, as he was in 1961, a singular anchor for hope and optimism.

"A titanic figure," one critic called him as his current tour began in England this summer. Dylan, changing pronunciations and exuding more urgency than ever, sang old songs with the new, including "Maggie's Farm" and "Girl From The North Country" at one outdoor concert before 250,000 English fans at Blackbushe.

Back in the United States, Woody Guthrie's most famous song "This Land Your Land," had become the theme of a Ford LTD commercial.

Dylan's Friday night Olympia concert will be one of the 115 on his international tour. Sixty-five of them will be in the United States. For many, it will be a visit of celestial importance. Two long years have passed since the mop-haired, harmonica-playing genius brought his Rolling Thunder review to Ann Arbor.

"You can be in my dream if I can be in your dream. I said that," sings Dylan, inviting everyone inside to that place where they have the option of seeing the Dylan that is themselves. An expected 15,000 fans will have the opportunity of seeing a living legend Friday night.

The legend began shortly after Dylan had arrived in New York City in 1960 and had begun developing a small following in the folk circles of Greenwich Village. Within that year, he was signed by producer John Hammond on Columbia records and began recording his first album.

"Who's Bob Dylan?" people asked as the scratchy-voiced minstrel emerged, smiling like a hip choirboy from the cover of that legendary recording. By

1962, when his second album, "Freewheelin" was released, they were saying, "Here's someone who can put it in words. He's got to be listened to."

What they heard were songs like "Blowing In The Wind" and "Don't Think Twice, It's All Right," everlastingly poignant folk-hymns that the group Peter, Paul and Mary had already popularized. As William Hedgepeth said, Dylan was able "to seize intuitively upon the aspirations and unlocatable pains hovering in the atmosphere and render them in a form for people to wrap their arms around." His songs, Hedgepeth said, "made ordinary life look different and caused people to ask questions about themselves."

Dylan's third album, "The Times They Are A'Changin," defined a generation in terms of its values and verbalized into consciousness the reality of changes in progress. The title anthem became the primary anti-Vietnam War fight song. One journalist said, "Today Bob Dylan is Shakespeare and Judy Garland to my generation. We trust what he tells us."

Dylan took his message on the road for five straight unstraight years, touring at first, by station wagon. To straight people along the way, his biographer Tony Scaduto says, Dylan "seemed on the edge of some dark cataclysm, totally unreal, always stoned, speaking in unintelligible parables."

Once, in the early days, his band's car was pulled over by a Colorado State trooper, after they had passed a funeral procession.

"What are you people doing?" the officer asked. "We're a group," Dylan said, holding up his guitar, "like the Kingston Trio, but there's four of us. We sing." Like his records, they were released.

With his next album, "Another Side of Bob Dylan," many began perceiving a shift away from topical material, viewing it as a loss of commitment. Others suggested that Dylan was becoming more certain of himself artistically.

Epic images had begun springing from his mind at this point, according to Scaduto, as Dylan delved into the writings of poets, Rimbaud, Brecht, Byron, Ginsberg and the anonymous authors of the Bible. He had become the source of pop music's unpredictability with his importance being first aesthetic and social and then as an influence.

His first hit single, "Subterranean Homesick Blues" appeared on Dylan's fourth album, "Bringin' It All Back Home," in 1965. The next album, "Hiway 61, Revisted," was acclaimed as "impossibly good" and proceeded the definitive Dylan recording, "Blonde on Blonde."

In the summer of 1966, following his recent bride, Sara, down a country road on his motorcycle near their home in Woodstock, N.Y., Dylan spilled, breaking several vertebrae in his neck and suspending his career for nearly five years.

During this time he made only three appearances, including a Woody Guthrie benefit, George Harrison's Madison Square Garden concert for people of Bangladesh and the second Isle of Wight Festival in England, where critic Jonathon Cott said he looked "like a mirage."

Recovering slowly, Dylan began recording in Nashville, Tenn., eventually releasing the fine albums "John Wesley Harding," "Nashville Skyline" and "Self Portrait." Having quit cigarettes, Dylan had begun singing with greater authority and with new tonal breath control.

Dylan never sounded more like Dylan than on his next album, "New Morning." Soon thereafter, he received an honorary doctorate of music from Princeton University. Subsequent efforts included the albums "Planet Waves" and "Blood On The Tracks" and participation in the films "Pat Garrett & Billy The Kid" and "Renaldo and Clara."

"Street Legal," Dylan's latest album, was released late this summer. One critic called it "a dreary affair." Another said that Dylan sounded "utterly fake." Most observers, however, felt the album perfectly represented the composite Bob Dylan, an artist who is constantly being reborn. As writer Jim Jerome noted, Dylan is an artist who "undeniably creates in a genre in which minimal art is almost impossible."

Poet Allen Ginsberg says that Dylan has grown up in recent years, saying, "he's alchemized a lot of the hang-ups of his past."

The late Ralph Gleason once said that classifying Dylan as a rock 'n' roll performer or a folk singer "is like comparing Isaac Stern to Evelyn and her Magic Violin."

Dylan says that the purpose of his art is to inspire others with the belief that they can also be creative. "I don't care what people think of me," he said a few years ago. "It doesn't concern me. I'm doing God's work."

Ode Boy! Area free-lance writer makes odes a way of life

Trudi Blake wanted to write the story herself.

"Be sure you put this in," she persistently instructed during a one-man press conference recently in her Farmington Hills home.

Here's some of what Mrs. Blake dictated should be in the story.

• Her golfing husband's nickname is "Ace," thanks to a hole-in-one he shot at Baypointe Country Club a few years back.

• Her 6-foot-3 son "grew up overnight to discover a blond and a Honda 750." Mrs. Blake likes the blond, but not the motorcycle.

• Robert Benchley is her idol. "He had the ability to write the most marvelous whimsy," she said without serving coffee, "and maybe through osmosis or something I've picked up a thread of what he wrote."

If so, Mrs. Blake may be on her way.

A self-described "sensitive, menopausal, recycled, loquacious, overweight, semiliberated and indigent, weary but hopeful wife, mother, inflation-fighter, free-lance writer who thinks she needs rejuvenation" – Mrs. Blake is also a self-described "odemaker."

An odemaker writes odes. Odes – according to Oakland University associate professor of English Jane Eberwein – are a rather unusual, difficult-to-define form of modern poetry traditionally characterized by seriousness, formal stanza structure and the heightened use of celebrant language.

"They're in the lyric category, but they're not narratives," Ms. Eberwein says, recalling the works of Shelley, Keats and Wordsworth.

Narrative or not, for Mrs. Blake odes have become a way of life.

"Written chronological verses is for me one of life's irreversible curses," she says, designating the line for specific inclusion in this story. The odemaker's easiest-to- remember "must include" line is, "I write image pieces," a point she stresses repeatedly. "That's very important. Be sure you use it."

Mrs. Blake's lyrical flights (image pieces called odes) celebrate vacation trips with Ace (her husband George), television's "Today's Show," The Grand Hotel on Mackinac Island and a visit to the dentist, among other personalized topics.

These are of equal seriousness to the odemaker. They also may help explain the need for one-man press conferences.

To promote her verse, Mrs. Blake – who also calls herself "the Motor City's Meter Matron" – solicits not only newspaper stories, but assistance from advertising agencies, university English departments, restaurants and publishing houses as well – in the name of advancing her work.

"At this point I need all the help I can get," she admits. "I just can't get started. Sometimes I get so discouraged I have to ask why it is I knock myself out all day writing odes. Let's face it, there isn't any way you can market poetry on your own."

In spite of this, her efforts continue, which may help explain the need for one-man press conferences.

"Why should Stan Freeberg be the only humor writer in the world?" she asks. "I want people to read my odes, too. With all the violence, sordidness and pornography in the world, people need the warmth and whimsy to placate them. I consider benevolent humor and goodwill catalysts that help keep sane heads on shoulders and attitudes bearable."

Yet no one buys Mrs. Blake's odes.

"Maybe people don't want to be uplifted as much as I want to uplift them," she says.

Newspaper editors tell her "odes are old stuff" and advertising executives say poetry has fallen on hard times.

"As to your hopes of marketing this particular style of writing on a free-lance basis to advertisers," J. Walter Thompson, Vice President, Kinder Essington, told Mrs. Blake in a letter after she'd mailed him a packet of odes last year, "I'm afraid you're fighting city hall and the mayor's name is Darth Vader."

Essington went on to say, "The notion of selling personalized odes to motivate people to buy a particular product would be rejected out of hand by most businessman. (And businesswomen for that matter.)"

He advised Mrs. Blake to gain advertising experience and sent back her odes.

"I'm not returning your material as a subtle form of rejection," Essington said. "I just figure it'll save Ace some Xerox money."

Businesswoman Jane Trahey of the New York City-based Trahey Advertising Co. told the odemaker of Farmington Hills, "I haven't a clue how you can go about merchandising such rare talents," advising that Mrs. Blake "try reading Phyllis McGinley, Judith Viorst, Ann Sexton, Ogden Nash, etc., just to get a feeling of other people's work in poetry."

Educators tell her they're too busy to help, or ask for $25 per hour professional fees. Rhymes written for restaurants such as the Bijou and Hogan's have all fallen on deaf ears.

"They're still trying to figure out how to use them," Mrs. Blake says. "I've suggested putting them on menus but they argue that customers wouldn't read them because they're too busy at lunch. They say their restaurants are too dark at night. I'm really amazed with their apathy."

After researching for months, Mrs. Blake produced an "Ode to Detroit," only to subsequently face a lack of interest from the city's Chamber of Commerce, Convention Bureau and mayor's office.

When she offered the ode to Detroit's city magazine, editor Gary Deidrichs replied, "If it's verse, don't bother sending it."

Agents representing publishing houses – Mrs. Blake says V either don't answer inquiries or, when they do, inform the suburban odemaker that "verse is a dreg on the market."

Or, as Robert Frost once said, "Proportionately, there is more poetry in the United States than any other commodity."

Despite the resistance, Mrs. Blake persists. Locked away in a quiet room neatly cluttered with bric-a-brac, family pictures and an electric Smith-Corona typewriter, her one-woman assault on the literary world proceeds.

In a recent letter to a newspaper editor she wrote, "I always think onward and upward when I write. Lately, I feel I have been in limbo. Not regressing, but not advancing either. Ace calls me his "Frustrated Writer'; says I will be the Grandma Moses of the literary world. I don't think I can wait that long."

And to the one-man press conference at her home last week she confessed, "It's getting to me physically and mentally, but I'm not going to quit. It's too satisfying. I'm still getting better. And who knows? Maybe I'll still write the ode that no one can resist."

We'll put that in the story.

After a 66-year odyssey, their joy is in 'just being together'

Oscar sat in his chair, ready to share a smile and a friendly comment with anyone who walked in.

Edna sat a few feet away, closer to the television. She had a book of puzzles in her lap.

"That's my hobby," she said. "I always have a puzzle workbook."

Oscar and Edna are the Baileys, originally of New Ringgold in Schuylkill County and now full-time residents of the Leader East Nursing and Rehabilitation Center, 200 Second Ave., Kingston.

On Tuesday, the Baileys celebrated their 66th wedding anniversary.

"We were getting married in New Ringgold on Thanksgiving Day, November 25, 1920," Bailey remembered.

"Then we took the train to Reading for the night."

Sixty-six years later, the Baileys remain together, in a small but comfortable room they've shared for about a year at Leader East."

On this Thanksgiving, the couple will give thanks for each other and for all the things in life for which they are grateful.

"You bet we will," Bailey acknowledged. "For just being together."

"Oh come on, we fight like cats and dogs," his wife said, kidding her husband.

Later, she set the record straight. "We had words but we never fought."

Bailey will celebrate his 91st birthday in February. Without exactly getting her permission, he told a visitor his wife is 85.

"Oh, don't say that," Mrs. Bailey objected.

"What's the difference?" he asked.

"OK, I'm only 16," she said. "At least I wish I was."

The Baileys' children, George Bailey and Jane Hartranft, both of New Ringgold, visit their parents as often as possible, as do the Baileys' six grandchildren. And during a typical week, other guests take time to sit with the Baileys and exchange tales and greetings.

On the day of their 66th anniversary, the Baileys had the pleasure of the company of the Rev. Wesley Kemp and a group of singers who came to the nursing home to entertain residents with music and prayers.

After wishing the couple a happy anniversary, Kemp remarked that after such a long marriage, Mrs. Bailey must surely be inclined "to hang on to" her husband.

"Uh uh," she said to Kemp with a straight face. "It ain't too late. I can still kick him out if I want."

Her husband did his best to conceal a grin.

"Actually, when I got married, I said I wouldn't leave him for no money," Mrs. Bailey said.

After he left, Mrs. Bailey said Kemp visits them nearly every day.

"The singers come every two weeks or so," Bailey said.

And when there are no visitors – which is most of the time – the Baileys still have each other, and their television.

Television, in their case, consists mostly of soap operas and what Bailey called "doctors programs," all of which blared from the couple's television set as the Baileys talked about their life in the nursing home.

"Heck, we're happy in here," Bailey said.

"We don't need to go out of our room too much," Mrs. Bailey added.

They said lunch and supper is served to them in a nearby dining room. Accordingly, that's where the couple will be today, eating turkey and possibly indulging in a small splash of wine before going back to their room.

Pittson Area High School ceremony takes on a family flair

Lou Harashinksi's great-grandfather Anthony Pasquerello had a son and three daughters. One of the daughters became Harashinski's grandmother and the son became Darren Minich's grandfather.

In tracing relationships like these, you could come to grips with the essence of the Pittston Area High School Class of 1986, which celebrated its commencement ceremonies last night.

The class of 1986 consisted of 330 graduates, six of whom had perfect 4.0 grade averages and another 40 of whom qualified for the National Honor Society.

Beyond the academic achievements, however, lay a greater familiar truth – approximately one-fifth of the graduating seniors from Pittston Area High School's Class of 1986 are linked together by family relationships.

"There's no doubt, we've got a lot of cousins this year," said the school's principal, John Donovan. "There aren't that many brother and sister combinations but there's a bunch of cousins."

Harashinksi and Minich – two of Pittston Area's 330 graduates – posed for multitudes of pictures this week with their cousins Michelle Musto and Larry Miller.

Other cousin groups bearing names like Calabrese, Menichini and Pesotine joined in the Pittston routine as the cameras clicked away during the days preceding the school's commencement ceremonies.

"It felt weird going all the way through school with this many cousins because none of us were good at the same thing," Harashinksi, 17, said.

For example, Harashinksi – the son of Louis and Gale Ann Harashinksi, 313 Simpson, Dupont – was a college preparatory student; his cousin Michelle was in general education.

On graduation night, none of this mattered.

"I think we're all going out tonight together," Harashinksi said, hours before his graduation.

Commencement opened with the proud members of the Pittston Area Class of 1986 filing through two rear gymnasium doors, the classes' 180 girls dressed in white gowns and its 150 boys dressed in either red or blue.

Amid blinking cameras and shouts of encouragement from friends and family, the graduates found their way past flags and floral arrangements to their seats.

Following a salute to the flag and the National Anthem, the audience heard the Rev. Julio Serra, pastor of the Mount Carmel Church in Pittston, ask God to bestow his favor on the graduates.

"Give them ideals and make their life beautiful," he said. "Above all, keep them in the palm of your hand, right now and in the years to come."

The graduates then heard their fellow student Jeff Bachman offer a class prayer. "Help us cherish memories of our friends," he asked.

Another student speaker, Anissa Burns, proclaimed, "We have reached our goal – graduation."

Outside the gymnasium, within earshot of the podium, an ad-hoc gathering of the Proud Fathers Society stood together, comparing notes.

'I had one last year, one this year and now I got two to go," said Edward Herron, whose son Robert sat inside among the graduates.

Another father, David Berlew, drew on a cigarette as his daughter Annie listened to a musical selection inside. "I've got six down and one to go," he chimed in.

"They can't wait to get out, but then in two weeks they really miss it," added an obviously experienced father named Mike Guzzy, whose son Richard was about to graduate.

Inside the gymnasium, the evening's ceremonies neared a climax when Dr. Anthony J. Mussari rose to deliver the commencement address.

Mussari – an associate professor of communications and history at King's College – received hearty applause when he assured the audience his remarks would be brief.

After noting that he could not remember a single word uttered by the commencement speaker at his own high school graduation in 1959, Mussari challenged the Pittston graduates to set out on one simple goal.

"Just be a good person," he said.

"Be a good human being. That won't get you on News- watch 16 or on the front page of The Times Leader but it will give you what every person in this room is seeking – personal happiness, contentment and peace…In spite of what any TV commercial says, just be what you feel comfortable being, regardless."

Frank J. Nardone, the president of the board of education, presented the beaming graduates with their diplomas.

Probing the presidential psyche

The American presidency, by all immediate indicators, appears to be enjoying one of its more manifest phases under the headstrong administration of Ronald Reagan.

Forget the scoundrels of the past. Effectiveness has returned to the White House. Let the business proceed.

Beneath the real-life surface, however, the American presidency is facing tougher times than ever. Credit the publishing profession.

The written word of late has been bad for past presidents. Very, very bad.

In particular, two bodies of recent work have surfaced in the area bookstores this fall, both suggesting that the office of the presidency in our country may now be attracting some of the most psychologically deficient individuals our society has to offer.

One book deals with former President Richard Nixon and the other with the late President Lyndon Johnson.

Perhaps the biggest blow to the notion of presidential sanctity came earlier this year when the W.W. Norton Publishing Co., of New York released historian Fawn Brodie's lengthy study, "Richard Nixon, the Shaping of his Character."

Examining Nixon's boyhood, Ms. Brodie portrays a lonely, narcissistic, distrustful young man who delights in acting, lacks a sense of real identity and is inclined to always be on the attack.

In this book, former Nixon White House lawyer Fred Buzhardt tells the author that Nixon was "the most transparent liar" he ever met.

Ms. Brodie has her explanation.

"Nixon certainly knew right from wrong, or at least legal from illegal and truth from falsehood. But he didn't care," she concludes. "He has no emotional investment in the truth."

From his Quaker beginning in Whittier, Calif. – " a small walled town resisting the enemy with its bastions of decorum and constrictions of the spirit" – Ms. Brodie's study follows Nixon through various abandonments, fantasies and failures to communicate emotionally.

"In Nixon's earliest years neither of his parents was able to communicate a sense of basic trust or of his own worth," the author writes. "The clues were wrong."

The reader meets Nixon's "myth-making" mother, Hannah Nixon, and the former president's punishing father, Frank Nixon. Later, the reader learns how young Dick Nixon develops a special talent for being "pretty convincing" to avoid that punishment.

Being "pretty convincing" the author says, is the same as being deceitful.

"Nixon feared and disliked his father as loud, brutal and sometimes dirty," Ms. Brodie writes. "But Frank was also preeminently masculine. For Richard to be cool, fastidious, and quiet was to be like his mother. He would put his mother's manners into the service of his father's objectives."

Meanwhile, as if all that's not enough, a sizzling portion of Robert Caro's new book, "The Years of Lyndon Johnson," which will be published next fall, appears in the October issue of the Atlantic Monthly magazine.

Caro's biography of Johnson, the 22nd such work to appear on the former president's life, described in great detail how LBJ went from being a dirt-poor politician from the woe-begotten Hill Country of southwest Texas to the richest man to ever occupy the Oval Office. The story is an enormously depressing one, featuring consecutive incidents of corruption.

Once in the presidency, Caro says, Johnson continued his wicked ways.

"Attainment of the presidency did not slake his thirst for money," the author writes. During his five years in office, in fact, Caro says Johnson personally directed his business affairs back in Texas by telephone, even though LBJ had ostensibly placed those affairs in a "blind trust" when he was elected to the presidency.

Not only did he deceive the public on this issue, Caro says, Johnson also pursued his personal business interests on the taxpayers' time "down to the most minute details, not infrequently working on those affairs…for several hours a day."

Even worse, Johnson used his personal power to wrench even greater favors.

"In his direction of his business affairs, he did hesitate to use the power of the presidency itself, and to use it with utter ruthlessness," Caro writes. "And during his presidency, Johnson piled atop millions of dollars he had already made (and) made millions more."

Caro says Johnson was consumed with ambition and ambition only and that the former president pursued his career with "the energy of a man fleeing from something dreadful."

Ambition, Caro writes, was not an unusual attribute for a young man in Washington D.C. in the days immediately proceeding the New Deal. But the author says Johnson's ambition was uncommon "in the degree to which it was unencumbered by even the slightest excess of weight of ideology, of philosophy, of ideals, of beliefs."

Johnson – who friends said, "had charm to burn" – is portrayed as "a wonder kid of politics" in his early days in Washington.

Beginning with a job as a congressional aide and extending into the period of his own legislative career, the portion of Caro's book that has been excerpted in the Atlantic Monthly shows Johnson developing the special "communications tone" that would carry him to the White House.

"It was a tone that would have been familiar to his college classmates who heard him talking to professors," Caro writes.

"For on Capitol, as on College Hill, he was as obsequious to those who were above him as he was overbearing to those who were not."

In college, in fact, Caro notes that Johnson acquired the nickname, the nickname by which he was identified in the college yearbook, of "Bull" (for "Bullshit") Johnson.

His fellow students, the biography says, believed not only that Johnson lied to them – lied to them constantly, lied about big matters and small, lied so incessantly that he was, in a widely used phrase, "the biggest liar on campus" – but also that some psychological element impelled him to lie, made him, in one classmate's words, "a man who could just not tell the truth."

Professional Sports: DOOMED

For owners, players and "members of the organization," pro sports is a business that provides an ostensible product – a competitive sports team.

For fans, pro sports is about tradition, civic pride and athletic excellence. Fans want their teams to win, even if the members of those teams appear to be more focused on the cashing of the check than in fulfilling fans' emotional needs. For sane observers of the professional sports scene, the challenge sooner or later is to come to grips with the fact that those two truths cannot forever coexist. Inherently, fans seeking real passion and players seeking real wealth are on a collision course. Expect a certain KER-BOOM any day now.

OK, you're a pro athlete. You have an agent, an attorney, an accountant, a broker, perhaps a public relations counselor or a full-time personal trainer. You're like a corporation. As such, there has to be a large degree of confusion in the part of your head where brains traditionally reside. On the field, you're scooping up ground balls or fouling off another 3-2 pitch. Off the field you're directing your millions.

To little Jimmy in the bleachers, you're a hero, a great big guy who can hit a ball farther than he can imagine. To Jim, your agent, you are the ultimate cash cow. Here come 'da owner and he is really going to muck this thing up. As an employer, 'da owner is instinctively inclined to pay you as little as possible. It's the American way. As the employee, your instinct is to get as much as you can, for as long as you can. Like every yuppie on a caffeine buzz, you want to acquire as many certificates of deposit as you can while your capacity to acquire still works. Like all of us, then, you plug on. And this is good. Before we get lulled to sleep though, do you still hear those trains heading toward each other?

For pro sports the dilemma is simple yet confounding. The fan is the key. As long as the fan buys into the premise that all is purposeful on the field, ice or court, the gambit will persist. The fan will pay to observe the spectacle, assuming the spectacle has, (from the fan's perspective) integrity. What happens when that perspective begins to dilute? Look around you. Massive cynicism sets in.

OK, you're a fan. Are you ready to plop down $75 to sit around with a bunch of impersonal snobs and see Shaq O'Neal miss a foul shot? Will you hide out in the sanctity of your boring house and watch one hundred meaningless football games this year? Will you drive downtown all winter to watch the Wings make the depressing playoffs?

If you answered "yes" to any of these questions you are exactly what wealthy owners need. While the game is being played, the owners know people like you and your dippy neighbor Walt will suspend logic and imagine that it means something.

Later, when yer back at home and you look at the standings and wonder why darkness is enveloping your mood, an appropriate sense of suspicion should be setting in.

Why? Because logic takes over again. Your brain reactivates. Walt's too. You begin to suspect that where "your" team is in the standing bears no actual relevance to your personal wellbeing or to the overall quality of life.

You get a sinking feeling. You know you've been had. Anger erupts.

Soon your brain is once again fully engaged. Atlanta beat Cleveland. How about that? You still have $17 in the bank. You owe VISA more Do-Re-Mi than Albert Belle makes in three innings. You're considering suicide. Pro sports isn't going to save you either, even if it is making owners and players richer than all of Mr. and Mrs. Bill Gates' unborn grandchildren.

It doesn't take the Rockettes seamstress to know the professional sports establishment needs to get real. As fans we are all disillusioned. You're too rich. We're too poor. Your spectacle will not always be our spectacle. There's too much Great Divide.

How often do you hear the Detroit athletes saying something genuinely passionate about the people of Detroit? You're right. Practically never.

In failing to commit to us the same way they expect us to commit to them, "our" players and owners are missing something very elemental.

If I can figure it out, why can't they?

Spook-tacular Uncle Ted is no stranger to TV

Ted Raub has only one more TV station to go and he will have completed the Scranton/Wilkes-Barre Big Five Cycle.

Hold on, you say. That's an event I never heard of.

OK then. How about Le Tour de Susquehanna?

Raub is commonly known as Uncle Ted on the Friday night WVIA-TV, Channel 44 program, "Uncle Ted's Monstermania" at 11:30 p.m. He has been a fixture on local TV in this country since the mid 1950s.

And, at age 66, he isn't ready to slow down. Not completely, anyway.

"Channel 38 (WOLF) is the only station I haven't been on so far," Raub said. "I don't think they're ready for me yet."

In due time it's bound to happen, unless the world goes completely nuts or some future president bans television. For one thing, you can't keep a good man down. And you certainly can't keep a good clown down, even if he does host monster flicks.

To understand Uncle Ted, you must know he is first and foremost a clown/entertainer. The horror bit has simply come with the territory.

Back at square one, in fact, Raub began as a substitute host of a kid's program on WBRE-TV, Channel 28. The show was hosted by an elf-like character named Mr. Nobody, who held forth with the youngsters on weekend mornings.

"I came in when Mr. Nobody got sick," Raub said.

"I was Professor Feathers. I'd never been on TV before, but it wasn't that hard," he said. "I just put together some stuff and made a costume using a pair of pajama bottoms with elastic on them, some nurse's white socks and a hat and beard. It was a ball."

Raub's first TV gig lasted three months, until Mr. Nobody got well.

"That led to unemployment," Raub joked.

But unemployment didn't last long, thanks to the fact that every TV station the area – and just about every one in the entire country, for that matter – produced at least, one local kid's show in the 1950s.

As a result, every local show needed an actor to serve as the clown-host or cowboy-host of these programs, which created enormous job opportunities for aspiring show biz- types like Raub.

" 'Captain Kangaroo' was the big thing then," Raub remembered.

On the local front, there were several equivalent characters, in addition to the Captain, Mr. Nobody and Professor Feathers.

For example, modern-day radio announcer Frank LaBar was known as Roscoe the Rascal, and served as host of a "Little Rascals" show on one station. And former television executive Tom Riley was Texas Tom on another.

Even radio executive Jim Ward was once a television character who was known as Buckskin Jim, Raub said.

After his brief fling on WBRE, Raub went on to perform on a kids show on WDAU (now known as WYOU-TV, Channel 22) and later on a horror show on WNEP-TV, Channel 16.

The transition from kids shows to horror show came easily for Raub.

"I kept doing basically the same kind of stuff, but with a different costume. I used the same tricks but with a different line of patter."

One of Raub's longest stints took place in the early '60s, when he hosted "Uncle Ted's Children's Hour" on the old WDAU. Raub, who was also a copywriter at the station, said he got the job because none of the station's announcers was interested in it.

"They didn't want to lower their dignity."

On the "Children's Hour," Raub played the records, coordinated puppet shows, hosted a regular magician and performed pantomimes for his young viewers, whose birthdays were celebrated on air.

"That's when I started putting money in the Swiss bank account," Raub kidded.

By the end of the '60s, he took a production job at WNEP where one of his bosses came up with an idea for what Raub now calls his current "monster bit." According to the scheme, Raub became host of a Friday night show called "Uncle Ted's Ghoul School."

On WNEP, Raub's shows were first produced live. Later, many programs were taped for subsequent broadcast, to accommodate the fact Raub had taken a simultaneous job with a Philadelphia-based entertainment agency.

"They needed a guy to do an ESP (extrasensory perception) act for high school assemblies," Raub said.

"I didn't know anything about ESP but I was able to fake my way through shows for them, even though I didn't take it too seriously. I could fake the bits because I set them up, which is not to say there isn't anything to ESP."

During this period, Raub said he made from 450-500 appearances a year, putting an average of 30,000 miles a year on his car. His work took him from New England to such western provinces as Ohio. He often performed three shows in a day. "Sometimes you'd luck out and get two in one school."

During these years, Raub began doing some of the most basic of magic tricks, which complemented the puppet shows and pantomime bits in his school appearances.

"I'm definitely not the greatest magician in the world," Raub admitted. "But the most important thing is to entertain people and I think I do that pretty well. If someone laughs, that's good. Or, if they turn you off, what the heck?"

Between the fake rabbits and rubber pigs, Raub has definitely kept on laughing, both on local TV and out on the hustlings.

He said he's done his comic-magic act in every imaginable setting, from nursery schools to nursing homes, from fairs to festivals, from church bazaars to firehall fund-raisers, from private parties to huge assemblies, from birthday parties to bowling banquets.

"You name it, I've played there," he said.

Raub said he is still interested in working although he seeks to control his schedule. "I try to pick and choose. I could never do three shows a day again. I have a nice home and do what I want to do. But I don't need to live high off the hog."

Raub lives in Dallas, in a house he's shared with his wife Angela since 1946. The Raubs are the parents of three children: Rita Kalinosky, 41; Beth Bassmer, 30 and Ted Jr., 38.

He began his current horror show engagement in Nov., 1985, when WVIA started airing a syndicated package of scary films.

Among the movies shown on the program this month have been "Black Sabbath," "Dr. Blood's Coffin," "The Vengeance of She," and "Prehistoric Woman."

Raub said he feels the content of the movies broadcast on "Uncle Ted's Monstermania" is dated but entertaining.

"They're corny but great," he said. "I don't like the modern-day horror films because they're too overdone with special effects. The old stuff had better story lines and plots. Plus, the good guys always won."

While he really doesn't mind the films he introduces each Friday night, Raub said he is a long way from being what you would call a horror-movie nut – a description that might better fit the many college kids in the Valley who watch his show and send him fan mail.

"A lot of guys think I'm really into these type of movies," he said. "I'm not, although some of them are so bad, they're actually good."

On the show, Raub wears an old tuxedo and a modified Shriner's hat and performs most of his bits on an impromptu basis.

When Raub was on WNEP, one of his regular viewers was a skinny teenager from Nescopeck named Richard Briggs, who is now a producer/director at WVIA and also performs as "Nephew Ned" on "Uncle Ted's Monstermania."

"I didn't even know they had television sets in Nescopeck," Raub said recently to the 33-year-old Briggs. For his part, Briggs said the time he spends helping Raub produce the show is the highlight of his job.

"All I have to do is act goofy, which isn't very hard," he said.

Raub journeys to WVIA's Pittston Township studios every three or four weeks. In the studio, he and Briggs tape openings, bridges and closing segments for three or four shows at each taping session. For the record, Raub said he is in it for the fun, not the money.

"If I told you how much I was getting paid for this, you'd wonder why in the heck I was coming up here. But, the truth is, I'm having a great time doing it. And that's what matters."

And abracadabra…there is another motivating force driving our Uncle.

"You always hear about the guy who always just wanted to play Hamlet, right? Well, that's like me. I've always thought, if I could just get one guest shot someplace…like on the 'Carson Show,' well, that would make my life."

And if that doesn't happen, well…there's always Channel 38.

Talbert: Modern Philosopher

Who looks like a cross between Mike Lucci and Norman Mailer, doesn't belong to the Press Club and went on a second honeymoon trip with his first wife the week before their amicable divorce?

If you answered Shirley Eder, you're wrong.

They are on the same page, occasionally, but the answer is Bob Talbert, Spartanburg, South Carolina's gift to Michigan's newspaper lovers.

Do you have the most interesting job in town, Bob?

"If I didn't have it, I'd sure like to have it."

Bob Talbert's daily column in the morning *Detroit Free Press* has been a hit in Motortown since John Knight lured the 41-year-old anecdotist from "The Columbia State," South Carolina's largest paper, in early 1968. "Being the top columnist is frustrating because I can't cover everything," he says, sharing the warmth of his Southfield condominium. "But the most worthy topics usually rise to the top."

As opinion makers go, Talbert is pre-imminent. His current liquid protein diet success has created a minor wave of interest around the metropolitan area, threatening to alter the course of his career. "I may start a syndicated nutrition column," he admitted privately, half-serious, half- astounded.

Talbert is living on the experimental edge of change.

"Some writers survive on style and a predictable view of the world," Talbert's boss at the *Free Press*, Gary Blonston says. "Talbert survives on his ability to shift with the wind."

Bob Talbert breezed into life on May 28 in 1936. Spartanburg had three colleges and a small town sophistication not altogether typical of the area. He hung out around newsstands, was high school student body president and played football with enough grace to ascend to Davison University on a football scholarship.

In freshman English 101, Talbert, who "had charmed my way through high school," encountered his first indications of intellectual awareness, discovering Mellville's "hidden meanings" in classic passages of Moby Dick. "I've been a slave to words ever since," he says.

Talbert was a sportswriter before joining the Columbia, South Carolina *State,* where he toiled as feature editor, Sunday editor and columnist for eight years. He came to Detroit after our long newspaper strikes and six months after the 1967 riots. His mandate from the Free Press was "to write a column that will appeal to the broadcast audience possible."

Upon visiting the American Oslo, Detroit, Bob saw hippies from Ann Arbor, thought that everyone in a suit was an executive with General Motors and bought a hamburger that fell apart because it was "a Coney." He loved the way cars merging on the freeways maneuvered. He was overwhelmed by the size of the place. "You could drive for 20 miles and see solid stores. I didn't see how any columnist could get a finger on as big a place as this."

His first summer in Detroit, Mickey Lolich, Denny McClain, Dick McAuliff, Mickey Stanley, Jim Northrup, Al Kaline, Norm Cash, Willie Horton, Dick Tracewski, Ray Oyler, Bill Freehan, Dick Wert, and others on the Detroit Tigers brought the city the World Series baseball title. "The victory was fantastic," Talbert remembers. "It was the finest social high I've ever been involved in. People really believed in themselves. It was beautiful. I'd like to see that spirit in Detroit again."

Talbert's voice trailed off into different chains of thought. "Detroit's had a rim job," he said. "You can write that down. We've got suburbs rimming the city like a doughnut. Maybe Detroit could become a bedroom for the suburbs. People could drive out and in instead of in and out."

The theory makes sense.

"We gotta' grits mafia' up here," Talbert exclaimed upon first arriving at the *Free Press*, long a bastion for southern-bred journalists. The Knight Newspaper chain, it seems, has a strong feeder system from the Dixie states, especially with powerful affiliates in Charlotte and Miami.

"All this about a tradition of southern writers is a bunch of bilge," Talbert drawls. "People who can write, can write, and people who can communicate, can communicate."

Talbert's been getting the words out to as many as 3 million readers each day for nearly 10 years now, establishing a familiarity with Michigan readers that has no equal, Dick Tracy and Joe Falls not withstanding.

At first, he took it easy. "People don't want the opinion today. They'll let you know when they think you've earned it."

Today he notes, "You never know what's 'gonna stir people up. For one thing, controversy and gossip are too easy. The hardest and most rewarding column is when you hit on a small subject that turns out to be more dear to people than you ever expected."

Most of the time Talbert writes what he chooses. Fast and prolific, his columns frequently reflect his personal life. "I try to cover all the beats," he says. "I'm trying to find out what people feel."

Free Press Sunday Editor Gary Blonston, who inherited Talbert in September, 1975 when assuming his current position, keeps track, in a cumulative sense, of what Bob "is too close to see." Blonston adds, "Bob's columns are directly addressed at people in their daily existence." A good columnist, he says, must have a good sense of all kinds of humanity and pay particular attention to the little things that happen in life.

The Instant Bob Talbert:

- I'm not intimidated easily and I'm not modest. Perhaps those are shortcomings.
- You have to have a mammoth ego to believe that anybody gives a damn what you have to say every day.
- People read me because I'm habit forming and I'm unpredictable.
- I don't believe anybody today has any idea what it's all about.
- We're the biggest hindsight nation in the world.
- My biggest problem is I can't say no.
- There's too much tension everywhere.

-   In 1968, I started coming to conclusions. I still think there's an international cartel that no one knows anything about.

Lynn Guyman graduated from Seaholm High School in 1966. Years later she phoned Bob Talbert because, she recalls today, She seemed like an approachable person. At his apartment later, innocently, Lynn spilled diet red soda on her shirt.

She tried to wipe it off, she laughs, lightly. "It was really queer." They met three times to discuss Lynn's writings, then Talbert asked for a date. "I didn't think that much about it. I looked at him as Bob Talbert the columnist. I didn't think of him as a person, just a picture in a small box."

Looking back, Lynn says that their meeting happened at a great time. Timing, she agreed, can so often be the key factor with these things. "It's so weird," she rhapsodized.

In November of 1975, Lynn and Bob were married.

"We lived together for seven months," Lynn says, "and decided to weigh the reasons to get married against the reasons not to get married. We couldn't think of any reasons not to."

Lynn runs down an incomprehensible scenario involving mothers and Florida honeymoons, coming up for breath with 'I was scared that married life would be different. It was. It was better."

Her husband shouts from several hallways away, "Marriage took the pressure off!" The southern accent lends a Talbert shout added authority.

"Bob's really conservative," Lynn continues. At 28, she is very pretty and open-faced, works for a freight-shipping firm in Southfield, and shops with Bob in Birmingham at Wilson's Drugs, the Little Professor and the Continental Market. They also enjoy Shain Park and the 1/16th mile-track at the Bloomfield Vic Tanny Club.

Bob wrote a column at the *State* in South Carolina. "It was more bucolic then," he recalls. "Folkier." People wonder how he can kick out so many columns in Detroit. He tells them about wearing many hats at a time earlier in his career. Do people understand?

"I operate on two or three different levels," Detroit's most familiar writer admits. "Sometimes when people are talking I write the things they are saying in mind…I sort of drift off a little bit…people think I'm going crazy…I'm just memorizing what they're saying."

Whatever's happening, Bob.

Somehow he keeps one week ahead of himself with his columns. "His work is fast and light," Blonston states with kind authority. "It touches a lot of people." Talbert writes at home, in his cluttered basement, away from the distractions of the editorial offices of the *Free Press* fifth floor where his desk sits prominently amidst serious secretaries and quietly aging intellects.

In the basement Talbert sits for bi-weekly six-hour sessions, pounding another week's copy. Earphones connect him to an elaborate tape system from which Marvin Gaye, Pink Floyd and Bob Seger resonate perpetually. "I play it as loud as it can be played," Talbert boasts, grinning like a musketeer between his expensive space-aged earphones.

Talbert has lost 40 pounds since Easter. He hasn't had any booze since 1963 when he weighed 310 lbs. Most days he would consume either 2 fifths or 3 cases of beer, if his memory is still to be trusted.

"Believability is all we have in the column business," he concluded. " Harry Belafonte once told Tommy Smothers," Bob Talbert once told a friend, "Don't Blow Your Platform."

Tommy Smothers blew his platform.

Bob Talbert doesn't intend to make the same mistake.

The art of collecting business cards

You never know when they'll come in handy.

That's why I've saved hundreds of people's business cards. You never know.

A promotion man for Warner Brothers Records I once met gave me his wildly shaped calling card, featuring a smiling Bugs Bunny chewing a carrot.

It's in my top drawer.

A nice lady I met in a not-so-nice place one night slipped me her card. It had a picture of a bird decoy on it.

"What's this?" I asked.

"My dad makes decoys," she said. "It's my dad's card."

She was a decoy for her father. Still, I kept the card. I keep 'em all. Cards are crazy.

I love mulling over them, especially the cards of my smug friends who have since gone out of business.

At Open Crate, Inc., a home-furnishing store in Southfield, owner Sheldon Freedheim's card is designed in the shape of a shipping tag.

Shellie's still in operation but I keep his card high on my stack.

One night I picked up a card at The Phoenicia, a Lebanese restaurant on Woodward Ave. in Highland Park.

Now, years later, the card's thin, bamboo-like surface – reminiscent of the restaurant's walls – is disintegrating as it sits enclosed by a rubber band in a stack of other cards.

I need to go back to the Phoenicia and get a new card. I love food. I also love cards.

Experts in the field say calling cards were first used in the 18th century. They were handwritten, often by professional penmen. Originally called visiting cards, they were left after calls were made to one's home.

"They were a potent way of introducing someone," card expert Frederick Schang told the Christian Science Monitor. "They testified to the verity of the person being introduced."

The tradition has weathered the winds of time. Everyone has a card now. I've saved zillions of them.

Folks don't necessarily show up in the order I met them in my card stack. I realized this when I found an interesting card of a woman from the Magic Mountain Herb Co. next to the uninteresting card of the president of Bronte Champagnes & Wines.

I met the Bronte man a few years ago between the wine racks at Alban's in Birmingham. He asked me to come over to Paw Paw to visit his fields. I might go someday.

On some cards, the designs used graphically befit the companies represented.

There is, for example, a buffalo on the card of Buffalo Builders of Ft. Collins, Colo. And a cowboy on a horse on the card of Al Righetti who operates the AAA Western Wear store in San Luis Obispo, Cal.

There are also the shapes of bugs on the cards of Volkswagen repair shops that I've patronized from coast to coast. Shirley Foote of Foote Realty in Clarkston has, yes, a foot on her card.

Ironically, though, the best graphic artist I know, a cynical guy named Charlie Shepherd, who works for a design company in Toronto, has a perfectly plain card.

Robert Karazim, who lived next door to a girl I once had a blind date with, slipped me his card. It said he worked at "Sir Real Estate."

Bob's card folded out. Inside it there was a space provided for note taking. Above that space was the bold inscription, "hear ye! hear ye!"

Bob said he might have his own cards printed.

Looking through a huge stack of accumulated cards, I found an interesting one given to me a few years back by an old college chum.

He had spent several years trying to start an import company. A lot of us wondered what was taking him so long. Finally, we learned, he was getting close.

He had, in fact, even reached the point where he was having his business cards printed.

That would take some more time, though, we were told. At least another three months. The cards had to be designed. That alone would take most of the summer. Then the right printer had to be found.

This friend never knew how many wonderful laughs were provided by the saga of his card.

I have one of those cards. It is a wonderful creation, complete with a margin in the middle where my friend signs his name when he presents it.

Sometimes I pick my teeth with the damn thing.

Speaking of picking, incidentally, after he had finally picked up his cards from the printer, our friend spent an entire week distributing them to all his acquaintances.

We'd been waiting anxiously.

"Here I am," he said, "on this card. If you ever need me, I'll be here."

Then he would leave. And not be there.

Yes, cards are crazy.

Executives from A-Square Studios – a recording and rehearsal facility in Ann Arbor – give strangers a fold-out card designed along a long wire that expands as you unfold.

Get the message? They have cords.

A chamber of commerce person from Traverse City has a card with a picture of a cherry growing off a pine tree. This is known as a keeper.

Another great card was given to me by a woman from the International Visitors Council of Detroit. It features a drawing of that city's famous skyline, sans Renaissance Center.

It may be the only drawing of its kind.

Still, the stories go on and on.

San Francisco real estate broker Michael DeLany's calling card is conceived like a monopoly card. Garvey Janitorial Service of Pontiac has cards featuring a hand cleaning a wall with a decorative blue sponge.

The card of Paws 'n' Claws, a pet grooming shop in Royal Oak, highlights a splendidly rendered sketch of a fox terrier.

I have two of those, in fact, in case someone would like to trade.

I happen to be looking for an original Trini & Carmens.

I even have quadruples of some cards from people who insist on giving me one every time they see me.

My brother leads the league in most-cards-given category. I understand his situation, though. Like most people in my family, he's in the insurance business.

My favorite card was given to me by a man named Enrique Villalobos.

I met the Mexican gentleman one warm afternoon in a park in Guadalajara, Mexico.

He works in the construction industry.

On this card, Enrique's name is framed within yellow goal-post-like lines. The card also has an aesthetically pleasing green and orange insignia on it.

In the insignia, the only word that remains visible is "cemento."

I doubt if I'll ever need much cemento, especially in Guadalajara. But I love Enrique's card.

And, after all. You never know.

The legacy of coal

Nolan. Levy. Nomensky.

The names of the merchants tell the story.

From Pittston to Duryea, the names on the signs atop the stores reflect the very soul of Northeastern Pennsylvania's anthracite culture.

Pagnotti. Stassi. Beltrami.

The names of the coal dealers also tell the story.

From Old Forge to Avoca, the names of the coal merchants reflect the past and remain the basis of the future of Coal Country.

The Pagnottis and Nomenskys came to the region in great numbers to help mine the coal that built the world we knew.

In the collieries and in the coal towns, they joined other immigrants, with names like Kurlancheeck, Parzych, Swantkowski, Capo and Tylawski.

Individuals representing 36 nationalities mined coal in Northeastern Pennsylvania at the turn of the century. And 70 percent of the 63,000 people in the region were foreign-born or born of foreign parentage.

Colonies with give-away names like Scotch Road, Murphy's Patch, Welsh Hill, Huntown, Little Germany and Little Italy dominated the landscape.

Little Germany and Little Italy are names from the past. Yet the Kurlancheeks and Swantkowskis remain.

Combined, the names of the various ethnic groups reflect the ultimate truth of the anthracite region – particularly the Wyoming and Mahooning valleys.

That truth is written throughout the region, in the names of its citizens and institutions, in its towns and villages, in its history and future.

Anthracite attracted a historically unprecedented multi- ethnic base of workers to the Scranton/Wilkes-Barre area, a demographic mosaic of hard-working people that to this day remains unique in the United States and the rest of the world from which this diverse mix of people came.

Because of coal, the people came. And many of their descendants remain.

The discovery of anthracite in Northeastern Pennsylvania forever changed the makeup of the area.

Coal put bread on the table and Wilkes-Barre on the map, it was commonly said.

It was true. Coal shaped the development and history of our region in a unique way. And the remnants of that past continue to shape our daily existence and our expectations.

"I've heard Wilkes-Barre referred to as 'Little Saudi Arabia,' because of the potential value of the existing carbon in our coal," said U.S. Congressman Paul Kanjorski, D- Nanticoke. "There are people who still believe we have the equivalent of a gold mine here."

And there are many who see coal as strictly a historic topic, a sad subject that is not relevant to the present or future tense.

The negative legacy of coal, they say, is better forgotten.

Nevertheless, anthracite remains the region's most abundant and unique resource. And new high-technology means of extracting it from the ground and from the hundreds of mountainous waste piles in which the valuable hard coal remains mired may allow Northeastern Pennsylvania to return to its historic role as an energy producer and exporter.

*   *   *

To get some idea of what our area would be like today if coal had not been found beneath its soil, you need only travel eastward along the Susquehanna River, through the passive hills and quiet farm country that characterizes most of the region beyond Wyoming Valley.

Outside the anthracite belt, you will discover, farming and lumbering remain the primary providers of income. But in the broad valleys where Wilkes-Barre and Scranton co-exist – the Northern Anthracite Field – hard industrial development and the population mass it attracted comprise the dominant influence.

It was true yesterday. And its truth persists, today and into the future.

Coal is the most complex rock on earth. And the cultural mix that emerged in the anthracite region of Northeastern Pennsylvania reflects an equally Byzantine pattern.

Coal lies beneath a third of Pennsylvania. More than any other raw material, coal shaped the state – its settlement growth, industry and landscape.

To this day, eight eastern counties in Pennsylvania have 96 percent of the 7.4 billion tons of anthracite reserves identified as recoverable by the U.S. Bureau of Mines.

The anthracite region comprises 1,700 square miles in Northeastern Pennsylvania.

Its richest strain – the Northern Field – stretches up Wyoming Valley and beyond Scranton, from Shickshinny to Carbondale.

It is the largest concentration of low sulfur anthracite in the world.

The proximity of coal to the markets of the eastern seaboard, the extraordinary thickness of the vein and its superb quality made the anthracite region the greatest coal producing area in the country.

That anthracite coal existed in eastern Pennsylvania was known as early as 1768 when coal was used in Wyoming Valley for blacksmithing purposes. In Wilkes-Barre, anthracite was burned in the Fell House on South

Washington Street early in the 19th Century, when the first mine companies were established.

When Wilkes-Barre was settled in the late 18th Century, it wasn't known that a tremendous natural resource existed just below the surface of its rocky topsoil. Instead, the city was established on its present site because of the scenic beauty of the territory, said historian Carl Corlsen in his book, "Buried Black Treasure: The Story of Pennsylvania Anthracite."

During the War for Independence, shipments of anthracite were transported by water to the Continental Armory at Carlisle, Pa. This coal was used by the American forces in their revolt against Great Britain.

By 1820, the local mining industry had truly begun to flourish.

With coal gaining acceptance as a domestic and industrial fuel, entrepreneurs formed companies to exploit anthracite fields and to develop transportation networks and markets.

With the entrepreneurs came the miners and their families and the development of the company towns, or patches, to homeowners and miners.

The isolation of the anthracite region ended with the coming of railroads. A multitude of different rail lines came in, linking the northern anthracite region to New York and the southern region to Philadelphia.

"We began looking to these metropolitan areas for our standards, both financial and otherwise," said Beth Jewell, curator of the Anthracite Museum of Scranton. "They provided a way to get out. For example, the Polish sent their daughters to become domestic workers for wealthy city families. A lot of our working class ethic was based on a cash need for money."

Immigrant groups lived in different sections of the new coal region and had a tendency to colonize in all areas of life, residentially segregating with their own fraternal and social orders.

Skilled miners from England, Scotland and Wales came first.

Coal had been mined in England since the year 1200 and many of these early immigrants came from long lines of miners, which helped them to assume positions of authority in the anthracite region.

German immigrants began arriving in the early 19th Century, followed by Irish settlers – 60 percent of whom spoke Gaelic – fleeing poverty and oppression at home.

"The coal industry itself became almost a microcosm of the development of the Northeastern Pennsylvania region," said Michael Clark, president of the Anthracite Industry Association in Washington, D.C.

The Welsh, primarily, were the ethnic group that owned and developed the coal communities, and Welsh workers did most of the work, until the arrival of the Irish, Clark said.

While the Welsh and the Irish were diversifying, Slavs from across southern Europe began taking over the main labor responsibilities in the mines. By 1910, the majority of anthracite miners were Poles, Italians, Lithuanians, and Russians.

A great mix of European peoples flowed to America, particularly after the passage of the Immigration Act of 1864, which made it possible to import workers under a contract similar to the indentured servant system. Mine operators sent recruiters to Eastern Europe to hire laborers for the coalfields. And even after the turn of the 20th century, agents went to the port of New York where they would prevail upon incoming arrivals from countries abroad to take positions in the hard coal mines.

Representatives of European nations brought their own customs and habits, their own ideas of decency and propriety, ideas that often differed widely. From the unprecedented mix of nationalities emerged strains of suspicion, misunderstanding and scandal.

In this context, competitive-minded mine operators sought to secure the required labor at the lowest possible wage rate, which – along with long hours and favoritism – irked the miners. It seemed the better paying and more responsible jobs were passed out to the English, Welsh or Scotch, with immigrants of Irish and German heritage getting the less important jobs.

Tension also increased because a considerable number of foreign-born immigrants were perceived as radicals and it was true many of them had been driven from their countries for political reasons.

All in all, the strain of mining coal within an intensely multi-ethnic group of not-entirely-ordinary people became indicative of the unique pulse of the region.

Northeastern Pennsylvania's coal culture shared many similarities with other principal coal regions of the world. But its mixed ethnic heritage set it apart from the rest.

"We developed differently because we imported our miners from a wide, successively changing number of ethnic sources," said Miss Jewel. "By doing that, we rendered ourselves close to historically unique."

*   *   *

In 1820, 365 tons of coal was mined in the anthracite region.

By 1852, after the arrival of railroads and canals linking the region with the eastern seaboard, the amount of locally produced coal jumped to 6,000,000 tons.

Within 20 years, the amount of tonnage shipped annually had reached nearly 23,000,000 tons,

Stabilization in the coal-producing counties of Northeastern Pennsylvania occurred between 1900-1920, when the anthracite region produced 80,000,000 tons of coal annually and employed 160,000 workers.

A comparison of employees engaged in coal and manufacturing in Luzerne County in 1880 shows that 92.2 percent were in coal while only 7.8 percent worked in manufacturing.

By 1904, immigration into the anthracite coalfields had begun to slow down.

Even during the halcyon days of the mid-1800s, the anthracite industry was a troubled giant, according to historian Charles T. Joyce, Jr.

"A headlong expansion of coal lands and collieries to meet the fuel and forging needs of the Civil War spawned rampant over-capitalization and tumbling prices soon after Appomattox," Joyce wrote.

Chronic over production followed, which further drove price levels down.

Toward the end of the 1870s, hard coal began to be replaced in the manufacturing sector by an even cheaper alternative – bituminous, or soft coal. By 1889, the industry's official organ. The Coal Trade, would announce that hard coal had become an almost entirely domestic coal.

Activity related to coal production continued to dominate economic activity in the area into the early 20th Century. But its lock was weakening.

In a history of Luzurne County compiled by the League of Women Voters of the Wilkes-Barre Area, several major events, which occurred in the 1920s, were cited as causes of the decline:

• During a six-month miner strike in 1925-26, coal users began to look to gas and oil as more reliable sources of fuel.

• Strict immigration laws passed during the decade cut off the supply of foreign miners willing to work for low wages.

• Increased taxes on coal companies reduced profits and led to unemployment.

• Miners became less willing to risk the danger of their work.

"The peak of hard-core production had been reached in 1917 and would never be reached again," wrote John Bodnar, in "Anthracite People: Families, Unions and Work, 1900-1940. "Traditional consumers had begun the shift to oil and gas and prospects were dim."

The immigrants who settled the Wilkes-Barre area forged a society, which was structured not only to take advantage of the work opportunities offered by anthracite mining but also to deal with the economic difficulties from which that industry suffered.

New arrivals – indigent – soon became bound to their employers.

"The age-old problems of capital versus labor were evident to economists of the day in the hard coal territory and a culmination of events developed accordingly," historian Corlsen wrote.

The growing irritation of the miners against the autocratic employers of that day led to the strike of 1842, the first recorded strike in the hard coal fields.

The first union in coal country was instituted in Schuylkill County in 1848, even though organizers had difficulties with numerous foreign-speaking, foreign- thinking prospective members. In 1861, the American Miners Association was formed and the United Mine Workers emerged at the turn of the century.

During the Great Depression, anthracite workers began to demand that the United Mine Workers of America (UMW) be replaced as their representative. They felt the union had made itself an ally of the coal companies, who for decades had controlled so much of their lives, their jobs, their lives, their local politics and their tax assessments.

"In fact," Bodnar wrote, "anthracite people held these companies singularly responsible for preventing other types of industry from locating in the hard-coal regions and competing with them for their 'captive labor.'"

In their book, "The Kingdom of Coal," authors Donald Miller and Richard Sharpless said an inbred group of coal entrepreneurs and lawyers maintained an iron grip on all- important public and private organizations and institutions in the area and even controlled both political parties. In doing so, these interests decided who would rise and who would fall, which companies would flourish and which would languish.

"In Harrisburg, they promoted the interests of Wilkes- Barre to the detriment of other rival cities such as Scranton," the authors wrote. "They succeeded in excluding outside investors from establishing industries not under their control."

Pressed with a slackening market for anthracite and strained by their disenfranchisement from the conservative UMW, anthracite miners formed an insurgent union, the United Anthracite Miners of Pennsylvania (UAM), which fought bitterly against the entrenched power of its old union as well as the local coal companies.

The UAM attempted to curtail operations at various collieries by stopping work themselves and by prohibiting UMW sympathizers from getting to the collieries altogether.

In one of the most graphic examples of the pressures of the time, mining families stoned the funeral procession of a miner who was killed while working during the 1935 strike. The next day, they filled the victim's open grave with tin cans and police officers had to be called to prevent the protesters from removing the body from the grave, according to a story in the Wilkes-Barre Record on March, 18, 1935.

The demands of World War I and World War II kept the anthracite industry going. But by the late 1950s, most surface mining operations were closed in the Northern Field and the intensity of anthracite production shifted to Hazleton and to the Carbon and Schuylkill county areas – or the 180-square mile Southern Coal Field – where an estimated 2,000-4,000 workers still find employment in the anthracite industry, depending on local and international market conditions.

Nearly all the anthracite in the southern field is extracted by surface mining – the method by which more than 70 percent of Pennsylvania's hard coal is now produced.

Reduced demand for anthracite and the emergence of new, competitive fuel sources helped spell the end of deep mining in the Wilkes-Barre area. And the Knox Mine Disaster of 1959 changed the status quo, perhaps irreversibly.

In the incident, miners operating beneath the Susquehanna River near Pittston and beyond a safety line that had been established to protect a calamity, accidentally collapsed walls and roofing of the Knox Mine on Jan. 22, 1959, allowed the river to flood all existing mines in Wyoming Valley.

Several factors contributed to the tragedy, according to findings published by a joint committee of the Pennsylvania Legislature that conducted hearings on the Knox Mine disaster.

The committee cited:

• Indifference and apathy on the part of the lesser, the Pennsylvania Coal Company, concerning the procedures for and the method of extracting coal.

• Incompetence of the supervisory employees of the Knox Coal Company.

• An incentive pay system that led miners and foremen of Knox to conduct operations without any regard for their own safety or position.

• Compete lack of interest on the part of the owners of the Knox Company in proper methods of extracting coal.

• A lack of qualified professional mining engineers on the staffs of both coal companies.

"These factors, coupled with a condition of nature – a rising, flooding river – set the stage for sudden tragedy involving the loss of 12 men who were part of the mining operation and for irreparable loss to the anthracite mining industry in the Wyoming Valley," write George A. Spohrer in the 1984 publication, "Proceedings and Collections of the Wyoming Historical and Geological Society."

Over 7,500 jobs in the mining and related industries were lost following the river disaster.

And indeed, the history of mining in the Wilkes-Barre area had virtually come to a close.

"There's a lot of anthracite still down there but it's not mine-able," Clark said. "It's either too deep or too close to the middle of towns. And don't forget, it was highly mined for over 100 years, so what's down there is not in a relative sense important."

According to most estimates, there were 20 billion tons of coal in the four anthracite fields before mining began. There are about 15 billion tons left – about 1,000 years worth at current production rates.

Because of the flooding that occurred, many feel retrieving the anthracite still buried beneath the Wilkes- Barre area would be impossible.

The cost of pumping the mines would be in excess of $1 billion and would take several years to accomplish. And if such pumping were to take place, Clark said, it would create a major subsidence problem.

Officials pondered a proposal to build a tunnel to drain mine water from the anthracite field to Chesapeake Bay, mainly to save the mining industry. The plan never went beyond the talking stage.

But not everyone has given up on the idea of seizing upon the remaining reserves of coal in the area.

Congressman Kanjorski, for one, favors continued underground mining of coal in Northeastern Pennsylvania. He said some coal in flooded underground mines could be mined by equipment developed for undersea mining and that other coal could be converted to natural gas underground without being mined.

Referring to "deep sea robotics," Kanjorski said coal can be mined underground and underwater in our region, without extracting water and without destabilizing the surface area.

He said technology also exists to convert coal in its current setting to methane gas.

"We stand at a transitional point, which I see as very optimistic and positive. Coal, energy and water will make Northeast Pennsylvania a very attractive area," Kanjorski said. He cited the innovative activities of the Pennsylvania Energy Development Authority, a vehicle for helping private companies finance projects.

"I think some exceptionally attractive things are happening. Those of us who've lived around the coal region in recent years have come to see coal as something of a disparagement to the area. Yet the truth is, coal could very well become the backbone and basis of a very exciting leap into the future."

Kanjorski said much will depend on how successfully technology, research and financing can come together. "The most significant thing happening is the fact there are now permits pending for at least 62 co-generation plants in the anthracite region," Kanjorski said.

"This will become a major electrical energy source and if properly controlled by the government, the area should become much improved ecologically over the next decade or two."

Deals to build three large culm-burning co-generation plants have been signed in Schuylkill County in recent months and three others are still awaiting financing, The Philadelphia Inquirer reported early this year. That activity is expected to mean more than half a billion dollars in new capital investment for the area.

The plants will operate with a new technology called fluidized-bed combustion in which anthracite culm is turned into steam and electricity. The cheap steam power is expected to attract different industries to the Pottsville area.

Bill Whitehead, a manager with Pennsylvania Power & Light Co., told the Inquirer that if the entire number of proposed culm-burning plants between Scranton and Dauphin County were to come online, they could together produce up to 500 megawatts of electricity, or about half the capacity of a typical nuclear plant.

"In a way, it's our forefather's savings account," Edward J. Dunleavy, a spokesperson for the Greater Pottsville Industrial Development Commission told the New York Times. "We just hope to compound the interest and take it out of the bank now."

Closer to home, a group called Culmtech, Ltd. operates a coal preparation plant in Jenkins Township. Modern technology at the plant separates still usable coal from the estimated 15 million tons of coal refuse, or culm, that remain in the mountainous banks in the area, which occupies a 212-acre site of three former mines: The Ewen Colliery, Inkerman #6 and #14.

Some of the previously discarded coal goes back to the turn of the century, said Culmtech Ltd. President David Small.

He said the culm banks consist of coal, as well as coal dust, slate and other extraneous materials which are removed from the high quality anthracite in the coal's process of passing through the breaker.

Small said raw culm is trucked within the site to a surge bin where it is fed via two chutes directly into a 7- story building. A computer-operated complex of massive machinery separates the coal from rock and dirt.

Small said the culm in its initial form enters into a mixture of powdery magnitude and water, which creates artificial gravity wherein the coal floats and the other matter sinks.

Continual recycling and washing processes then separates the valuable magnetite from the coal. Additional steps are taken to size the coal, before it is sold to brokers, who in turn market the Pennsylvania "Black Gold" to consumers in the region, utility companies and other buyers.

The development of another culm processing plant in Hanover Township is under consideration, but the opposition of area residents may slow its emergence.

"There's coal all over the place but people won't let you dig or blast anymore, so it doesn't make any difference," said Joseph Kutchka, 63, a long-time coal industry observer who lives in Jenkins Township.

"That's why coal will be extinct in the next 20 years. There's just too much money around now. All the old people made their money in coal. They just got too smart for it."

Kutchka, like other coal industry insiders, said strict state and federal regulations are also taking their toil on the industry.

"They're putting everyone out of business," he said. "They keep raising the bonds and changing the rules and ultimately, you just can't operate."

Thomas Lynott, grandson of an immigrant miner and current director of the Anthracite and Community Development Institute at Wilkes College, echoed Kutchka's sentiments.

"Regulations are holding up an industry that wants to move ahead," Lynott said.

"Mine operators have to deal with up to 11 different agencies and at least 9 or 10 different laws now. So you take and look at a guy who's going into the business today and he's got so many bloody laws and regulations to deal with that it's almost impossible to survive. This is really a difficult business."

The fear of fines and regulations has made the average mom & pop coal operator "gun-shy," Lynott said. "The average guy just can't keep up."

The Wilkes College anthracite institute attempts to assist the anthracite industry by improving the market and by serving as a liaison between the industry and government. The institute also conducts research aimed at addressing many of the pressing problems currently faced by coal producers and users.

"It is our hope that through research we can establish new technologies, techniques and standards which will alleviate many expensive problems and allow anthracite coal to again become a sought-after energy source,"

Another principal organization that is trying to promote the industry is the Anthracite Industry Association (AIA).

Formed in 1980 by Michael Clark, a Pittston native who served for many years on the staff of former Congressman Dan Flood, the AIA is a group comprised of the leading anthracite producers, distributors and equipment manufacturers. Last year, the organization launched a market development campaign to educate heating decision-makers about the benefits of Pennsylvania's "black diamonds."

The market campaign stresses anthracite's advantages over other energy sources. It extols anthracite's convenience, economic virtues and its low sulfur content.

"Anthracite touches people in one way or another almost every day of their lives," AIA proclaims in its marketing campaign.

The association boasts anthracite is used in everything from ink pens to the production of electricity. As a source of carbon, anthracite has been used in carbonizing steel and in the fining process of glass. It is also being used by water treatment facilities for sewage filtration. Although anthracite is primarily used for heating, it is also a key source of carbon for a variety of industries.

Carbon from anthracite is used in gas producing, telephone transmitters and even in the generation of electricity.

"We're trying to give our industry a national identity," Clark said.

Promoting anthracite in Northeast Pennsylvania is another of the association's major activities.

"We're still largely misunderstood in the region," Clark said. "People in general don't seem to appreciate our heritage, our current contribution and our potential. It's treated as a dead industry, which is wrong."

Seen against the past – say the year 1917 when 100 million tons of anthracite was mined in the region – the present annual production rate of 3.3 million tons may seem insignificant.

Nevertheless, to countries like the United Kingdom, Canada, Brazil and parts of western Europe, anthracite is an important product which is used primarily for space heating and to a lessor but important degree for metallurgical purposes.

Begun in the early 1960s, a U.S. Defense Department anthracite program in which hard coal is shipped to Armed Forces installations in Europe has made the government the largest consumer market for the anthracite industry. The program, which involves at least nine Northeastern Pennsylvania anthracite operations, is the result of legislation which guarantees that the Department of Defense will buy U.S. anthracite and bituminous coal.

According to the AIA, the contract has provided basic job protection in the anthracite fields for many years, enabling smaller companies to remain in business while providing larger firms with the necessary contract base for larger hard-coal production.

To people like Louis Pagnotti III, anthracite also remains an important product.

An engineer with his family firm, Pagnotti Enterprises Inc., Pagnotti remains seriously involved in the business of anthracite.

"We're still mining around Hazleton, but everything we mine has been deep mined before, so a lot of what we're getting is stumps and pillars," Pagnotti said. "This remains a risky business."

Pagnotti Enterprises is also involved in cable TV, insurance companies and excavation.

"We're in the reclamation business, ultimately," Pagnotti said. "Ninety-eight percent of the time we're moving rock. Less often then we'd like, we're in the coal."

The family company builds roads and bridges and was involved in the construction of major elements of the new North Cross Valley Expressway north of Wilkes-Barre.

Rather than sending men beneath the earth to get coal, modern coal companies like the Pagnotti-owned Jeddo Highland Coal Company operating near Hazleton rely on huge equipment to do the job – like a building-sized monster shovel called the 8700 Marion. The machine is 20 stories high and has huge buckets capable of moving more than 3,000 tons of overburden an hour.

"It's really a job to get this stuff out," Pagnotti said. "We use old charts to locate the coal. They're pretty thoroughly documented but most of them are no longer accurate. When they were closing the mines there was no real incentive for keeping good records. We're lucky to get 25 percent of what's still down there."

Pagnotti said strip mining often takes months of digging just to reach the anthracite bed.

In spite of the problems attendant to strip mining and the uncertainties still facing new culm-burning projects, the future of coal in Pennsylvania remains bright.

"The qualities and varieties of Pennsylvania coal are almost unmatched in other countries around the world," wrote Gov. Dick Thornburgh in the introduction of a brochure designed to attract international customers to the state's greatest resource.

"We have a vast and well-developed transportation network designed to deliver coal to you promptly and economically. Our workforce has outstanding skills and talent, developed from a long tradition of coal mining in Pennsylvania, and it possesses technical know-how to guarantee an uninterrupted supply of economical energy to meet your needs."

In the letter, Thornburgh said he is excited about the new interest in coal.

"Remember, we want your business because Pennsylvania coal is our heritage and your promise."

The marriage without any broken noses

Trying to get a straight answer from Jack Farrell is enough to exhaust the curious urge.

Farrell, 59, handles questions in a way that is anything but serious – even when asked to comment on his 23- year marriage to his wife, Shirley.

The Farrells, who live at 20 Midland Dr. in Dallas with their five children, agreed to discuss their methodology for matrimonial success.

"There's no secret to it, really," Farrell said. "You just smile a lot and put up with the things you have to."

A visitor didn't have to look far to understand the remarks of Farrell, who functions by day as the immunization representative for the northeastern district of the Pennsylvania Department of Health.

As the discussion surged in the dining room, four of the Farrell's brood of five occupied the nearby living room, relaxed in various poses before a static-ridden television set.

Daughter Mary, 18, was away at the time.

Ann, 21, a senior at Bloomsburg State University who is home for the summer, was vying for the use of the telephone, resisting the demands of brother John, 19, a student at Penn State's Wilkes-Barre campus who, it should be noted, had just strained a shoulder muscle in a motorcycle accident.

Patrick, 13, and Jamie, 14, were sprawled out on the floor, seemingly oblivious to the conflict raging about them.

Shirley Farrell – like thousands of times before – entered the fray, imposing temporary peace with the precise authority of the matriarch.

"I don't allow things like that to bother me," her husband commented as his wife returned to the dining room table. "If I get ulcers it's only because I'm worried about her getting ulcers. She's extremely conscientious on things. In 23 years, there's nothing I could do to change her."

Acceptance comes easily, Farrell said, when you're lucky enough to have married the right woman.

"I must admit, from my youth there were so many girls who wanted me," Farrell said with a straight face but with a give-away glint of deceit in his eyes.

"No, really, when I met Shirley I knew she was the girl for me. There's a certain knowledge that you know what you'd like to have."

The Farrells were married in Wilkes-Barre on June 23, 1962, following a 10-year courtship. "She could take me for a little while at a time, but then she'd say, 'This is too much for me,'" said Farrell, a 1944 graduate of Coughlin High School. "I think she knew she was my No. 1 when I gave her the first ride in my new '55 Plymouth."

Both Shirley (the former Shirley Evans) and Jack were in their 30s by the time they finally tied the knot.

"Our kids give us a hard time about that," Mrs. Farrell said. "They say if we'd started earlier they'd be older now. We basically ignore that."

Postponing marriage may have contributed to their success, although neither of the Farrells would agree to the possibility.

"Our feet were planted pretty firmly because we were older but I think you go through the same things younger people do," Mrs. Farrell said. Her husband re-entered the conversation. "The big thing is the monetary thing," he said. "It can trip you up if you allow it to."

A workable formula has been established in their family to help avoid such fiduciary stumbling, he said. Mrs. Farrell pays the bills.

"She stays on the case. I've always been a last-day man."

Such differences in personality, Mrs. Farrell noted, may be one of the primary keys to their happiness.

"I've seen a lot of couples who were alike and they seemed to clash all the time," she said.

"If there's anything wrong with our marriage, it is that we don't have arguments," Farrell added. "You'll notice I don't have any broken noses."

A moment later, Farrell said it had taken him three years to complete a certain paint job in the family home.

"I'm not too much for saying, 'I want this done now,'" his wife explained, as Farrell ducked into the kitchen to fetch another round of refreshments.

"You laugh, you cry, but there's no way you can put a dollar value on the blessings of having children," he said upon his return.

"You have all these fears when they're growing up, but then you see the cohesiveness of the family and you know it's all worth it, even though you've spent half your life screaming at them trying to get them up to bed."

A scratchy chain of dialogue continued from the television set in the adjacent living room as the dining room conversation began to wear down.

"My advice to young people getting married today would be to roll with the punches and be willing to talk," Farrell said. "We talked but I think we could have talked more."

His wife said she believes in the effectiveness of pre- marital counseling, as provided by various churches and other organizations in the area.

"Someone's got to tell them that life is not a bowl of cherries," Farrell said. "It is only what you make it. You can come up with apple pie or sourdough. It's up to you."

And what, Jack Farrell was asked, has he come up with?

"I'm eating pie everyday," he answered, serious, perhaps, at last.

The Pontiac Five still insist: 'We're innocent'

Bob Miles was a persuasive figure 10 years ago. Friends say that's the main reason he got into trouble.

Trouble is probably the best word to describe what came down upon the so-called "General" of the group of men who became collectively known as the "Pontiac Five."

Educated, articulate and – as one of his fellow defendants calls him to this day, "a born agitator," – Miles had emerged as the natural leader of what was in the 1960s a precinct level George Wallace campaign organization. That nucleus developed into a Klu Klux Klan group, with Miles becoming the grand dragon of the Michigan Klan.

When it came to finding the person or persons responsible for the Pontiac school bus burnings of 1971, none of the above did much to help Bob Miles – or the other four men among the Pontiac Five.

Miles and the others continue to deny any involvement with the bombings. But they've had to accept the fact that they were convicted in connection with the episode.

"I can accept the realities of life," Miles says now, looking back on the consequences of his political profile during one of Pontiac's most volatile political periods.

"I was perceived as the leader. I was the lightning rod so I expected to attract the light."

Along with Wallace "Woody" Fruit, Dennis Ramsey, Alexander Distel and Raymond Quick, the presence of Bob Miles attracted the light in a big way. He was accused in 1971 and convicted two years later on charges of conspiring to bomb the buses. He served six years in various federal penitentiaries – mostly at Marion Federal Penitentiary in Illinois – and will complete a three-year probation this spring.

Now graying at the temples, Miles continues to project a uniquely compelling personality. Actually, very little is different with the general of the Pontiac Five.

It can be said that Miles, now 56, isn't as eager as he once was to prove his point. Now Miles is content living as life he compares to "living in quiet exile."

That existence finds Miles and Dorothy, his wife of 34 years, living and working on a small farm near Howell in Livingston County. Rather than being obsessed with resisting the system or changing the world, Miles says he is now preoccupied at home with a tractor that always seems to be in need of repair.

The Miles are like many couples their age. Their daughter and son – age 14 and 10 at the time of their father's arrest – have grown up, married and moved away. Middle life has passed. Now another phase awaits. And one thing is certain. It will be difficult for the events in Bob Mile's future to compare with those he's experienced.

Raised in the state of New York, Miles came to Michigan in the 1940s after a stint with the foreign service and with the military. He says that by the late 1960s, he was earning up to $25,000 a year as manager of the branch office of an insurance company. Miles became president of an insurance executives' association, in fact, and was finance chairman of the Republican Party in Livingston County in 1966.

"The press never talked about those kinds of things because it isn't what they want," Miles says, recalling his experiences with the print media in the early 1970s. "It doesn't sell newspapers."

Miles was jailed in 1973 and released in 1979. He says he worked every day in one metal shop or another while in prison.

"I did the whole shot. And I was never paroled. They'd say when the other prisoners were getting paroled that they wouldn't be letting me out because I was a racist, which is a crime they say is worse than rape or murder.

"So they'd let the more violent criminals out which became pretty easy to understand. I mean, they were the repeaters, the guaranteed customers who they knew would be coming back in a matter of time."

Miles doesn't often express himself in anything less than three paragraphs; his mind apparently doesn't work that simply. And rather than avoiding a topic, Miles dissects it in depth.

Whether it's the parole process, the Pontiac Five or the state of prison reform in Michigan, Miles waxes consistently authoritative and eloquent. And his polemic flows like political poetry in its natural state. Consider:

• On the subject of the Federal Bureau of Investigation (FBI), the agency Miles blames for his incarceration:

"The FBI hasn't changed a bit since 1971. They were whores in the beginning and they're whores to this day. They betrayed our rights and the rights of everybody in this country, all for profit.

"This country is the Kingdom of Entrapment. Look at Abscam and some of their other projects. That kind of activity should be a thorn to every freedom-loving person in this country – but it's not.

"My concept of police organizations is that they're here to prevent crimes, not create them. But here we have the FBI, one of the largest secret police organizations in the world, spending all their time performing entrapments and trying to ensnare honest citizens.

"I think that's garbage. That's like the Soviet Gestapo. The only difference between the FBI and the KGB is one's like a street hooker and the other's more like an up- town call girl."

The average FBI agent, he says, is "amoral" and has "no belief in anything."

- On the subject of prisons:

"Prisons don't work, regardless of what you think about criminals. From a moral perspective, they make no sense. They're the most counter-productive thing we've ever come up with. Do you think if I pack you into a can of sardines it's really going to improve you?

"Think of this: instead of being sent to prison for six years, suppose the five of us had been sentenced instead to spending our nights and weekends repairing buses or working in some way on inter-racial relationships. Which would have been more beneficial for society? That or putting us in prison with bank robbers and counterfeiters who can teach you a trade?"

- Regarding busing:

"The emphasis should have been on the upper class with all the higher education and social awareness. But instead, the pressure was put in the areas that were least able to understand what they were trying to do. They went where the economic pressure was the greatest on the people and those people just couldn't handle it. And they haven't. They just moved away.

"If the bussing programs were so good, why couldn't the upper classes have taken the initiative? Then, when the poor people could see what a blessing the program was, they'd have been knocking down doors to get involved."

- On the subject of Jerome Lauinger – the Pontiac fireman who became an unpaid FBI informer and penetrated Miles' organization:

"If he (Lauinger) was reporting to them (the FBI) every other week they would supposedly have known what we were going to do. So why didn't they stop it? Agents should have knocked on the door and told us to stop it."

"When the FBI moved in it was after the fact. Where were they from the start of the supposed conspiracy?

"If the FBI knew this was coming down from the start, don't you think they would have had some cameras and reporters out there that night?

"Lauinger was supposedly reporting 'info' to them from the inside but he couldn't have been reporting because there was nothing to report.

"But once the incident (bombing of buses) occurred, the FBI in effect told Lauinger what to say. I can understand it now. He (Lauinger) was 'in the bucket' himself. That is, they had something else on him. It's called, 'switching the heat.'

"He was trapped himself. He never had a choice."

• On the potential societal value if the racial awareness he has gained:

"I'm interested now in dropping all the other areas (of political interest) and setting up a committee to consider alternatives to prison. But I'm not sure anyone's interested. Actually, what I really think is that all the experience is wasted now. I don't think there's any point in going out and trying to put it into use. People are too hung up with the KKK stereotypes. They're more worried about economic issues."

Though he says the public probably doesn't want to hear what he has to say, Miles still finds himself saying it – to a public that's willing to pay him up to $1,000-per- appearance.

Miles lectures primarily at civic clubs and high schools for two-hour sessions. He says he talks for an hour then answers questions during the second hour.

"I've never failed to be asked back again to any where I've lectured."

Nevertheless, Miles says he doesn't encourage lecture activity.

"I tell most people I want $1,000-per-lecture. It's a polite way of saying, 'I don't want it.'"

Miles also says he has avoided talking with the press. He says his discussions with an Oakland Press reporter – conducted in anonymity at rural Livingston County truck stop – was only the third interview he has granted since leaving prison.

"Bob talks pretty strong but he's gentle as a pussycat," one of Miles' old friends had said. It seemed true.

During the nearly three-hour talk Miles revealed an easy manner. Notably gracious with waitresses as well as his persistent companion, Miles seemed more like a radiantly intellectual middle-aged college professor than a convicted bus burner.

Miles says the public still has the latter image.

"On the lecture circuit they usually expect me to come in bare-footed with one overall hanging down. But I normally wear a three-piece suit or something like that. So much for stereotypes."

In prison, Miles says, he had plenty of daily exercise and "a lot of good sleep." As a result, he says he came out of prison in better shape than he was then he went in.

Miles says he is now ghost writing for a living. "I don't do anything or go anyplace else otherwise," he says.

His probation period ends in April.

Miles says he now shuns Klan activities. "I prefer clan with a 'c' rather than Klan with a 'K.'" He says he is out of touch with the other members of the Pontiac Five.

"Each of us understands that we're like ships that ride together for a while in a convoy but eventually move off separately in time."

Miles says an avowed Klan member from the downriver area of Detroit confessed to the bombings of the Pontiac school buses from his deathbed in an Ann Arbor hospital in 1974.

Miles and the others were in prison at the time and their attorney did not file the necessary papers at that point that may have earned new trials for the five.

"He admitted but to the Feds, that meant nothing. They had us on a conspiracy charge."

Miles said an FBI agent said to him at the time of the man's confession, "It doesn't matter whether you're guilty or not. All that matters is, you fought us."

The term "you" in this case included Fruit, Ramsey, Distel and Quick. All but Ramsey continues to live in the Pontiac area. Only Fruit was willing to discuss his current perspective on the occasion of the 10-year anniversary of the bus bombings.

"I'm trying to stay out of this thing now," Fruit says. "I already have three strikes against me in the ballpark of life so I don't see any reason for getting into the paper. People won't pay any attention anyhow. They never do until it happens to them."

Like Miles, Fruit continues to deny his involvement in the bus bombings.

"I didn't do it. None of us had any part in it. We'd been picketing and marching and I guess they just had to have someone to blame and we were railroaded right through. They claimed we were organized but there was no way we could have been, not with the little group we had. It was all garbage. Baloney. But we served our time, even though we didn't have anything to do with any of it. We were just scape-goats for them."

Fruit served four years in over 25 penal institutions in cities like Texarkana, Texas; Leavenworth, Kan., Sandstone, Minn., Oxford, Wis., Terre Haute, Ind., and Lexington, Ky.

Ramsey served an equivalent amount of time while Distel and Quick – who had been dubbed "foot soldiers" in the conspiracy – each served six months.

Born and raised in Kentucky, Fruit served in the Marine Corps and came to Michigan in 1957. Like Distel and Quick, he is married and a father. All three men are involved in business locally.

Like the others, Fruit says he continues to blame "someone on the inside" for being responsible for the Pontiac bus bombings.

"I'll always believe it was one of the branches of government, because they're the only ones who had anything to gain from it."

For Fruit, the experience was far from grateful.

"They (FBI agents) ransacked my house to pieces when they arrested us," he says. "They came in like gangbusters, shoved my wife and kids around, took all my tax records and left everything in shambles. And they never put nothing back. It was like some western or something."

It's bye-bye Birdie for fake Fidrych

Mark "The Bird" Fidrych, Michigan's multidimensional baseball hero, lay in a Henry Ford Hospital bed Thursday recovering from surgery that repaired torn cartilage in his left knee.

"Gee, I've never been injured before," the former ace of the Pierce Gas & Oil Station of Northboro, Mass. had said repeatedly following a flight north from Lakeland, Fla. the night before.

Across town a contest was being held. Twenty-four "Bird" look-alikes, chosen from over 200 entrants, gathered in the lobby of the Detroit News, eyeing each other anxiously. The flock would soon be reduced to six by a distinguished panel of media stars scrutinizing their curls, the ability to their walk and their bubble-gum snapping abilities.

But with "The Bird" disabled, the hunt for the ultimate Fidrych duplicate seemed more like a wake. Two dozen spitting images of the most exciting player in baseball sat quietly staring into space with consolidated concern.

I had never heard of Fidrych until last July. I had returned home from California, where I had spent five years trying to hack out a career as a singer-writer.

One night I headed for what had been a neighborhood grocery in my hometown of Birmingham. I found it had been converted into a restaurant-lounge. Awed, I decided to stay for a beer.

Before I was able to find a seat, a middle-aged woman approached me asking, "How are ya, Mark?" I looked around, assuming she was speaking to someone else. There was no one else around.

Attempts to convince her that I wasn't named "Mark" were unsuccessful. A California driver's license with an unmistakable photo and the name "Trout Pomeroy" plainly printed made little difference.

In fact, the situation was becoming uniquely uncomfortable.

Finally two men approached and asked if I wasn't really named "Mark." By this point I was nearing hysteria. "What's going on?" I demanded. "My name isn't Mark. Mark my word." They became confused.

"Are you sure you're not 'The Bird'?" one of the men insisted.

I didn't have any idea what he was talking about. Gulping my brew, I bade a hasty farewell to their mysteries.

Soon, of course, I learned of the remarkable, irrepressibly enthusiastic Fidrych. His uncomplicated, unpretentious nature struck a nerve with me, as it did with millions of other sports fans.

Unlike most others, it was my fate to pass the summer of 1976 as a "Bird" look-alike. Day after day the minor dramatics of a newspaper writer's life were diminished by an endless sequence of mistaken identities, all linking me with this unprecedented phenomena of the baseball world.

When the Detroit News announced their contest my telephone began jumping off the hook. Friends were calling, urging me to enter. There was nothing to lose, they argued, and it might give me an opportunity to meet the flaky ballplayer himself.

I knew that I had to ask myself some fundamental questions. Which comes first, wackiness or curls? Where else but in Detroit, with its collective inferiority complex and nutty Dick Purtans and Sonny Eliots running around, could someone like "The Bird" cause such a flap? And, most importantly, could I win the contest?

It was clear that the moment of truth would come early. As soon as the 24 semi-finalists were gathered, I knew, the obvious winner would be evident to all of us. By wearing a Levi-jacket and keeping my mouth mostly open, I expected to quickly demoralize the competition.

At the Lindell Athletic Club, where I paused for a burger before walking over to the contest, a young customer from Canada told me, "I think you look just like the sucker."

Confidence rising, I entered the Detroit News lobby. A small crowd of culturally starved star-seekers stood behind intense television lights. In front of the lights were assembled a collection of the most mop-headed Bird-types any fan could imagine.

Four of the contestants were young girls, three of them in Tiger uniforms. All were popping bubbles.

Mary Ann Lawson, a cute 15-year-old from Detroit, methodically threw a ball into the oversized glove on her undersized hand, hoping to convince someone of something.

Almost all the semi-finalists had Fidrych-styled hair, yet one rather casually clad lad had a clear advantage. Every move he made, every line on his face and hair on his head suggested "The Bird." I knew that my time was up and that his had just begun.

I wasn't among the six finalists.

I discovered that his name was Ken Badertscher, 20, of East Detroit. He isn't a particularly super baseball nut, which puts him in the same category as Mark Fidrych, who reportedly had never heard of the all-time single season home run king, Roger Maris.

Ken is a student at Detroit's City Barber College, which, it turns out, is central to his uncanny resemblance to Fidrych. Up until the announcement of the look-alike contest, he had many things in common with the zany hero, style-wise. But his hair was "usually pretty straight with a lot of body."

The hair presented problems until fellow students Kathy Emedi and Lynn Hicks convinced Ken to undergo a "water-perm" to curl his hair.

"These chicks set me up," he said with a Yankee draw.

And what a job they did. All the other semi-finalists were mumbling about Baderstcher as he was chosen as one of the six finalists who will appear early next week on local television for the final selection. The winner will attend the opening day game, compliments of the Tigers and the paper.

Back at the Lindell, Kathy, Lynn, Ken and I sat down for a beer. "Do you know who you look like?" Kathy asked me.

"Harpo Max," I said.

"No," she replied. "You look like Robert Reid, that father on "The Brady Bunch."

Maybe someone should start another contest.

The Stuff Myths Are Made Of

The luckiest people in the world in the summer of 1976 were Detroit Tigers fans. No, we didn't win the pennant that year, let alone the World Series. No one broke any of Babe Ruth's records. Overall attendance figures weren't that spectacular. Why then, you must be wondering, was this particular summer different than any other in the troubled life of your average Tiger fan?

The answer, my friends, is blowing in my brains. Twenty years have nearly passed but the memories of one of the greatest seasons in Tigers' history will never diminish in Semi Fan's beer-ravaged cranial cavity. To a large extent I am still there…out in the upper deck in left field…hysterically screaming my guts out along with 50,000 other totally amazed fans as Tiger's pitcher Mark "The Bird" Fidrych DOMINATED our imagination and the opposition.

Wild, wacky, and practically possessed was The Bird – the name his teammates gave him because he looked like the wildly tussled "Sesame Street" character. He was indisputably the most amazing phenomenon in American sports in the summer of our Bicentennial. The entire drama played out right here in southeast Michigan, igniting a degree of fan enthusiasm rarely experienced across America's fruited plains. Eventually, the entire country caught on to Fidrych- manic-mania.

• Bubbles-- Fidrych took bubble-blowing to new circumferences. It must have taken ten pieces of bubble gum to create the massive concentric apparitions endowed by this amazing pitcher as he circled the rubber, working himself into an apoplectic state before issuing the next pitch, which more than likely was a low strike.

• On His Knees -- Fidrych would get down on his knees and work the mound like a dedicated landscaping major. He'd move sand, pat it down, whisk dirt off the rubber, virtually worship the ground upon which he toiled. Was it theater? Of course not. That's why we went nuts. "The Bird" was the real thing. He wasn't acting, he was just being himself. His incredible self.

• Talking To The Ball -- In today's age of super-jaded TV sports, false sports, phony garbage and other overkill, it's touching to recall that as recently as 20 years ago we had the real thing, right here in our very midst. Yes, this spectacular pitcher talked "to the ball." He admonished the ball to do his will. He established a personal relationship with the ball. The ball would be HIS ball. The ball didn't have any choice. No one else in baseball paid any ball such respect. As a result of these efforts, Mark Fidrych coaxed great results out of the balls he first befriended and later pitched. Detroiters realized early on that The Bird was real. Zanier than hell, but real as could be.

• Darts At The Bottom Of The Strike Zone -- Mark Fidrych had a glorious 19-9 record in 1976. Nobody cold touch him. I can think of no other pitcher in baseball history with a greater knack for throwing low strikes. His memorable slants were rarely above the knees. He came at you from all angles. His control was uncanny and his speed was beyond exceptional. You could not hit the sucker. He owned the American League.

• The Hair -- Mark Fidrych was no traditionalist. Not only did he behave like a madman on the mound, his uncontrolled mass of ultra-curly hair was a huge mind blower in its time, thatching out from underneath his cap and cascading in multiple directions like massive modern art. • Foam At The Mouth -- The excitement that accompanied the Fidrych phenomenon was beyond anything this old word rat could possibly convey. Mere phraseology seems inadequate, oddly repulsive as a means to covey what really was. Words are ultimately cheap compared to actuality. The actuality was, when Fidrych pitched, Detroit went nuts. You had to go nuts. Fidrych was so unique, so electrifying and entertaining, so absolutely riveting that to do anything other than freak out when he was on the mound was to flirt with pure cultural irrelevance.

Fidrych made the team in 1976 at the last minute and wasn't a factor in the first few months of the season says Jim Hawkins, Tiger beat writer for the Free Press from 1970- 1982. By June Fidrych was the talk of Detroit. By July the whole country caught Fidrych Fever following a nationally televised Monday Night game against the Yankees in which Fidrych not only blew away opposing hitters, he also captivated American with his inexplicably precious personality.

In the summer of 1976, I had adapted a free-flowing hairstyle and people mistook me for Fidrych thousands of times. Eventually, I began signing autographs, just to get rid of people. I'd write "Mark Troutrych" of "Fid The Mark Birdroy." I finished in sixth place in the Detroit News' Mark Fidrych-look-alike contest. A few years later I attended an event at the Silverdome with Mark Fidrych. It was the only time we met and someone snapped a picture.

Mark Fidrych was unbelievable. The problem was, you had to believe what was happening because he was indeed alive and all of us did take place, "live," right in front of our eyes. It wasn't a dream, even though it begins to seem that way, 20 years later.

The sage of Mark Fidrych had a bittersweet ending. Following his astounding 19-9 rookie season, this pitching sensation from Northboro, Mass. faded from prominence.

Fidrych appeared in 11 games in 1977, three games in 1978, four games in 1979 and nine games in 1980, when he retired from professional baseball. He has remained a cult hero of sorts whenever Tiger fans gather. He goes to the fantasy camps in Lakeland. "He's still a character," Hawkins noted. "He's loved by everybody in the organization. He's just a genuine guy."

Looking back 20 years after the Fidrych phenomenon, Hawkins theorized The Bird's short run at fame may have contributed to his lasting legacy. "Had he continued to play there's a good possibility we might not even be talking about him right now," Hawkins said. "He had the meteoric rise and the meteoric fall. That's the stuff myths are made of."

To get if off your chest, put it on your chest with a T- SHIRT

Four-year-old Sean Callahan stood there, a plain T-shirt in his hands and tears in his eyes.

"He was upset because he couldn't tell the front from the back," his father recalled.

"He'd never seen a T-shirt without printing on it, so he couldn't figure out how to put it on."

Indeed, an entire generation of little Sean Callahan has come of age since T-shirts began appearing in colors other than white and with names, messages and designs on them, rather than opaque nothingness.

Callahan's grandfather, Paul Callahan, remembers the boring white T-shirt and the traditional period when the pioneer gave away to its first variation – a plain white T-shirt with a blue ring around the collar.

Among Valley residents, Callahan is something of a T-shirt guru, having been in the business of printing things on shirts for more than 20 years.

Now 67, Callahan got his start in the design field in the 1930s, when he worked as a sign painter for the Triangle Shoe Co. in Wilkes-Barre.

In the early 1960s, he and his son, Paul Jr., became partners in a shirt business, Calmar Specialties, Inc., 205 Main Street Luzerne.

Their timing couldn't have been better.

"We hit the big college fraternity push pretty good," Paul Jr. said.

Or perhaps the college fraternity push hit them.

In either event, Calmar was there in the early- to mid 1960s, when college kids and their many imitators led the charge of the T-shirt Revolution.

Fraternities and clubs wanted their names and insignias printed on T-shirts, sweatshirts and eventually from towels to paddles to banners.

Colleges themselves had long promulgated their worthiness, heralding their emblems on decals, notebooks and bumperstickers, as well as on all forms of shirts.

Sub-groups like the Theta Zetas and the Mu Now Zos took over, fueling the fires of the printed T-shirt craze.

Then there were the sub-sub groups, like individuals, for example, or small businesses or softball teams or bowling leagues – all captivated by the thought of getting their name or message on shirts.

Before you knew it, printed T-shirts had taken over most of the civilized world.

"Now you've got T-shirt culture all over, no matter where you go," said Paul Callahan, Sr.

To verify this, take a few moments someday and stroll over to the Army & Navy Outlet store at 113 N. Main St., Wilkes-Barre.

Since the early 1970s, team coaches, athletic directors and club organizers have ordered their special shirts printing from stores like this. And thousands of consumers have followed suit, asking for names like Reggie Jackson, Jimi Hendrix or Dr. J to be printed on the shirt of their choice.

"In the early days when we were printing, people wanted to emulate anyone that was cult and had a following," said store manager Sheldon Block. "They just had to have their name and number on their shirts."

In addition to letters and numbers, stores like Army & Navy Outlet store began offering print transfers in the mid- 1970s, when the big demand concepts were usually in beer motifs and humorous designs.

The film industry presented many of the themes that would grace the second wave of mega-popular T-shirts.

From the unforgettable picture of an angry shark rising out of the water in "Jaws" to the slim sexuality of the bleach-blond actress Farrah Fawcett, Hollywood's largest images became the hottest-selling T-shirts.

Other American cultural heroes would come to the T-shirt later, including William "The Refrigerator" Perry, Bruce Springstein, Mr. T and Rambo.

And few will forget "The Fonz" or the "Ghostbusters" insignia.

"Michael Jackson was also a tremendous T-shirt mover," Block added.

"But not as big as 'Ghostbusters.' They still ask for that, believe it or not."

Current winners include "Alf," Max Headroom and unicorn figures, Block said.

As slogans go, the clever-cut local favorite is the message: "Heaven doesn't want me and Hell's afraid I'm going to take over," according to various T-shirt dealers in the area.

Interestingly, shirts with dinosaurs on them have not caught on locally, although the national popularity of dinosaurs is one of the major success stories of the year.

At Spencer Gifts in the Wyoming Valley Mall, today's T-shirt fare consists primarily of I Felta Thi/Tappa Kegga Beer-type concepts and other derivations.

At his store, Block said shirts with Chevrolet Camaros on them sell much better than shirts with Pontiac Firebirds.

As concepts go, the sky appears to be the creative limit when it comes to thoughts on shirts.

"There are enough ideas out there to last maybe through the next century," Block predicted. "There always seems to be new ideas."

The examples are countless:

• After Bernard Goetz shot four teenagers in a New York City subway, the big demand was for vigilante shirts.

• An older man recently ordered shirts printed with the message: "Ladies, I know I'm Ugly But I Have Money."

- When toxic fumes were released from a burning building in Nanticoke, forcing the town's residents from their homes, shirts proclaiming "I survived the Nanticoke evacuation" began popping up around the Valley.

- A young man was spotted wearing a shirt that read: "Darn, I was going to get a job today. But I forgot."

The ideas, of course, go on and on.

"T-shirts have become like an adaptation of the old bumper-sticker," said Jim Howell, senior marketing analyst with the economic services division of the Memphis-based National Cotton Council.

"The only difference is now people are putting their message on their chest instead of the back of their car."

Howell said statistics indicate the amazing growth of the printed T-shirt concept has helped lead the way to a healthier cotton industry in this country. He cited figures compiled in 1985 by the Bureau of Census of the U.S. Department of Commerce that show printed T-shirts (T-shirts made for outerwear) leading among all categories of sport- shirts.

In 1995, more than 238 million such shirts were manufactured in the country, exceeding the number of men's lightweight T-shirts produced during the same period.

"And most people in our field suspect that a lot of the regular T-shirts eventually find their way into the outerwear T-shirt market, through fairs and sidewalk booth- type sales," Howell said.

However you slice it, T-shirts are big business.

Scott Gilbert, a commodities trader based in the heart of cotton country in Lubbock, Texas, said the cotton industry has experienced increased demand in recent years, partly because of increased T-shirt sales.

Army & Navy Outlet manager Block said overall T-shirt sales at his store have increased ten-fold in recent years.

"The funny thing is, white has remained one of the most popular colors, along with black and red," he said.

Block told of a lady who buys design T-shirts for her dog.

At Calmar Specialties, Paul Callahan, Jr. told of a client who recently ordered a number of shirts with apparently meaningless lettering across their front: when folded in a certain manner, however, the shirt's lettering bore an obscene message.

Dainty or dirty, you can choose your message from an increasing number of sources. Or you can adapt a message from somewhere else.

At a new kiosk in the Wyoming Valley Mall, a small retail outlet called Touchdown Sportswear offers printed t- shirts that bear the names of hundreds of far away schools like Clemson and Florida State University, alongside basic "I'd Rather Be Fishing"-type shirts.

"You can get shirts that say Italy, Moscow, Ireland, Scotland or just about anyplace," store manager Julie Betancourt said. "It's great. I mean, just because I wear a shirt that says Paris, it doesn't mean I was there."

Parting Shot

Just because I wrote these articles, it doesn't mean I was there. And even though my T-shirt says "tomato sauce", it doesn't mean I had pizza for lunch. Not today, unfortunately.

No, today I had the pleasure of re-reading these old newspaper pieces for lunch, along with a bag of trail mix and a small dollop of Rush Limbaugh. I urge every reader to rise to your feet immediately and extend Heather Wilson a rowdy round of applause for locking herself to a pc long enough to transcribe this work into a readable format. Thanks again, Heather!

Was it worth the effort? I think it was. If she had not re-typed this material, it would still reside in a file drawer, abandoned, forgotten and surely never again to see the light of day. It deserved a better fate. For it amplifies the fact any newspaper writer crazy enough to endure ten years in the journalism pit is bound to have at least 30 encounters with topics capable of retaining interest, years after the chewing of the fingernails. If these articles aren't timeless, my name is not Betsy Ross.

Like baseball players and other established thugs, writers need first to believe in themselves and only later to believe in their bookie. If I hadn't thought I was any good at this, I would have stayed on the food truck. Instead, I was careful about what I decided to be, knowing I would become my own personal vision, like it or not. For one decade, I poured my soul into being a good reporter, only to conclude after ten years in the saddle I'd be better off in the automotive training industry, where even children are assigned their own locker.

Older now and looking for a men's room, I can see "one brief run" as just that – a sprint of sorts, a mad dash to whatever stories would justify another week's crumby paycheck. I was lucky – I had some juicy assignments. Better yet, editors in desperate search of fast copy allowed me more than once to write columns, which drew more on imagination than they did infatuation. Between those two categories, I found my fair share of quasi-artful moments, favorites of which I've included within.

So then, to Rogers Worthington and Joe Stebbins and Tom Walsh and Larry Laurain and Alison Walzer and all the other editors who watched over this space cadet from 1976-1987, I thank you from the bottom of my Thesaurus for letting me go ape without putting on a monkey suit. To everyone enjoying this last lap around ego-dumb, I appreciate your willingness to help make this a two-way experience.

Doc Trout
August 2003

Transcription Notes

Writer Heather Wilson transcribed selected clippings from former newspaper reporter Trout Pomeroy's files. (That's me). She also was asked to write the following after- thought to this collection and was assured her words would be published, unedited, as part of the project. To say I appreciated Heather's effort would be like calling the second coming of Christ a relatively significant event. Without her help, this was just not going to happen. Every bit of her energy was required to transform a large stack of dated newspaper articles into one coherent mass. Heather completed the task with elements of her brain intact, proving you can fuel some of the peepholes, nun of the thyme. While moaning was heard from the next room, by the next morning, the room was vacant and all the symbols were embossed in computer format, there to be repeated for all womankind, for all time, immemorial and otherwise. Thanks again to Heather Wilson and Julie Cronenwett for your help in assembling this mass of work and your encouragement along the way. Thanks also to the readers of the newspapers that employed me and to the editors who massaged these pieces and gave me the opportunity to blow illegal smoke rings around the feet of their offspring and other neighborhood children.

Here, then, is Heather's artful inclusion.

Fourth coffee, wrinkled pants, pencil-stained palms, chewed pen, blood-shot eyes, trunk full of notebooks, business card pile-ups, newspaper-littered backseat, no time, no time, passed deadline, approaching deadline, irritated editor, irritated reporter, writer's cramp, writer's crap pay, writer – reporter – journalist.

I imagine we have driven down the same roads, as reporters, with five minutes to get to that press conference that started five minutes ago; to meet with that public official whose name has escaped our memory, or who is simply an ass hole that never gives us a good quote, or that 'Good morning' look he always flashes to the Channel 7 gal.

I know we've shared in the complete exhaustion that comes with a 50-plus hour workweek, for which we'll receive a lousy paycheck and lousy benefits. We know it's the kind of job that leaves the weekends for laundry and resting, and all the crap we never got to during the week because there were too many township meetings, last-minute stories, evening community events, and that in-depth piece we took on because we knew our co-reporter would approach it all wrong.

And I would bet regardless of the pay, the hours, the over-editing by editors, the rejection of our genius story ideas, and all the bullshit that comes with being a newspaper person, you would not trade a minute you've spent working as one for the world, or any other job for the matter. No, for some reason we like this shit – and from what I've gathered, it seems that we agree no other job is more rewarding than that of a writer – reporter – journalist.

Thanks for making me want to be one all over again.

-Heather J. Wilson-

www.ingramcontent.com/pod-product-compliance
Lightning Source LLC
Chambersburg PA
CBHW062010280526
45787CB00005B/2051